A Cookery Book
of Wild Foods

by

Sylvia Boorman

WILD PLUMS
IN BRANDY

Expanded Edition

Illustrated by
R. T. Lambert

McGraw-Hill
New York Toronto
Montreal
London Sydney
Johannesburg
Mexico Panama

WILD PLUMS IN BRANDY

92656

1 2 3 4 5 6 7 8 9 10 BP-69 8 7 6 5 4 3 2 1 0 9

Library of Congress Catalog Card Number – 75-100049

Printed and bound in Canada

TO MOTHER

*who first gave me a taste for flowers
by putting narcissus bulbs instead of onions
into the shepherd's pie.**

** Mother didn't know they're
very bitter – and poisonous.*

The author thanks the following for permission
to quote from books that they have published:

CONSTABLE AND COMPANY LIMITED
(*The Gardener and the Cook*, by Lucy H. Yates)

UNIVERSITY OF TORONTO PRESS
(*Bella Coola Indians*, by T. F. MacIlwraith)

THE MACMILLAN COMPANY OF CANADA LIMITED
(*Early Days in Upper Canada*, by John Langton)

CONTENTS

INTRODUCTION

In Canada, we do not have to go out to the fields and woods to gather and make use of every edible thing, plant or animal, that the land produces. So that this book is really written only for fun: for those people who enjoy roaming the fields and woods for mushrooms, who are pleased to have pots of delicately-flavoured wild berry jelly to give as gifts to friends; who prefer a trout caught and cooked the same day (if not the same hour) to frozen fish.

There are people who say "but why *bother* picking wild berries and getting scratched and hot in the sun when you can buy berries, all picked and clean – and much bigger – at the fruit store?"

This book, of course, is not for them. It is for you who can smell wild raspberries through the dust of a country road even before you can see them; or can close your eyes and recapture the heat of the sun and the sweet smell and the wild rare flavour of the strawberries you picked in long-gone summers.

You may find wild raspberries, say, growing in such rich profusion that you pick and pick far more than can be consumed with cream for tea; or you come upon a magnificent specimen of a puffball while walking through a meadow and feel it would be almost indecent to leave such a generous gift of nature to rot to a brown puff of smoke. On the other hand, some gifts of nature – like the trillium – it would be indecent *not* to leave, when picking means destroying the plant completely. There are some things, like trilliums and lark's tongues, which are preferable in their natural habitat no matter how great a delicacy they may be on one's plate or to one's palate. And when you come upon a clump of wild leeks, or a cluster of mushrooms, always leave some behind to reproduce another year.

WILD PLUMS
IN BRANDY

CHAPTER 1

Wild fruits

wild red cherry

grape

wild plum

crabapple

blueberry

Wild fruits

"The year or two after a fallow has been chopped, and logged, and cropped, in all the corners of his rail fence, and by the rude road that he has hewed out to his dwelling, spring up the red raspberry, black raspberry, the blackberry and often the strawberry. The wild gooseberry, both smooth and prickly, is seen on upturned roots, at the edge of the clearing. Wild currants, both black and red, are found in moist swampy spots: here also are often to be found wild plums and chokecherries, (the last not very fit to eat;) and a tangled growth of wild grapes, near creeks and lakes; fox and frost grapes entwine the trees, near the shores of lakes and rivers, while the high-bush cranberry shows its transparent clusters of scarlet berries from among the fading foliage, or on the utterly leafless bough."
Mrs. C. P. Traill: *Female Emigrant's Guide* (1854)

Many of the good things come all at once. Late last summer in the Kawartha district we saw wild grapes growing along a rail fence and hanging from trees. When we stopped to gather them, we found that the trees were wild cherry trees and

chokecherry bushes, and the purple grapes intermingled with the bruised red of cherries. So we picked a bagful of each, our hands stained purple and red and our faces covered with dust and cobwebs. But the jelly we made was worth it; the grape jelly, slightly tart, was a delicious accompaniment to our meat dishes all winter; the wild cherry was sweeter and was used on toast or hot biscuits; the chokecherry was used for both. They all made interesting visiting gifts, too.

It is highly satisfactory to get a lot of jelly-making done all at once, but make sure that you are well stocked with jars.

Blueberries

Of course, you can buy blueberries in the shops in the city, or at stands along country roads. But like all wild fruits, they taste incomparably better when you pick them yourself, warm and plump with the sun and eaten then and there. I myself never liked blueberries until I picked and ate them, idly, from low bushes along the shore of a small Laurentian lake.

Once you or your children start picking, you are likely to end up with brimming baskets of them. Having eaten a handful raw, sprinkled them on cereal for breakfast, served them in bowls with sugar and cream for dinner, what on earth are you to do with the pints and pints left over?

A friend of mine made an ambrosial meal of them this way: she baked a batch of tea biscuits before breakfast. (A kindly thing to do; she didn't use a biscuit mix either – but one could.) Hot from the oven, they were put on the table with a dish of berries, a bowl of sugar, and a jug of cream. We each put a biscuit on the bottom of a cereal dish, covered it up with blueberries, and covered *them* up with cream.

There is always a special thing about food when it is con-

nected with special times. We acquire violent likes and dislikes because of associations. It often takes a lot of talking to yourself to become convinced that a food dislike is utterly silly and childish; that you probably haven't even tasted the detested food since you were six – if ever.

But it is good to have the pleasant associations. So, for me, my friend's blueberry dish. Let me say that her house is halfway up a hillside overlooking Halifax harbour, and we are holidaying. It is also one of those rare mornings when no fog spreads over the harbour; the fog-horn is noticeable because it is silent. Only an occasional toot comes from small boats plying the sparkling water. A cream-soaked-biscuit-and-blueberry breakfast will always for me be a dish for a hot lazy summer day.

Then of course there are blueberry muffins for tea, and blueberry pancakes for breakfast or lunch.

BLUEBERRY MUFFINS

1 quart blueberries	*1 cup milk*
1 tablespoon butter	*½ teaspoon salt*
½ cup sugar	*2 teaspoons baking powder*
2 eggs	*2 cups flour*

Wash and dry the blueberries. Cream together the butter and sugar. Beat up the eggs and add them to the sugar, then add the milk and salt. Sift the baking powder and flour and add them to the mixture. Dust the berries by rolling them in some flour and stir them gently into the batter. Then pour the batter into greased muffin pans and bake in a hot oven (450 degrees) for about half an hour.

BLUEBERRY PANCAKES

You probably have your own recipe for pancake batter, or perhaps you use a mix. In which case, just flour the blueberries and

stir them into the batter. However, in case you have neither handy, here is a recipe:

1½ cups flour	1 cup milk
3 teaspoons baking powder	3 tablespoons melted butter
½ teaspoon salt	¼ teaspoon vanilla
⅓ cup sugar	1 cup blueberries
1 egg	

Sift together the dry ingredients. Beat the egg and add it to the milk. Then slowly add this liquid mixture to the dry ingredients, stirring until smooth. Add butter and vanilla. Flour the blueberries and stir them into the batter. Then drop by spoonfuls on to the griddle or into the frying pan, which should be fairly hot but by no means sizzling. You may serve them with maple syrup or golden syrup, or with butter, brown sugar, and lemon juice.

BLUEBERRY PUDDING

1 quart berries	2 egg whites
⅔ cup granulated sugar	3 teaspoons icing sugar
6 slices buttered bread or toast cut in fours	

Mix the berries with the granulated sugar. Put a layer of toast on the bottom of the casserole, and spread with a layer of the blueberries and sugar. Then repeat with a layer of toast and so on until the dish is full, ending up with toast as the top layer. Bake three quarters of an hour in moderate oven. When it is finished, beat the egg whites stiff, add the icing sugar and cover the top. Brown in the oven for a few minutes.

UPSIDE-DOWN CAKE

Combine a half cup of brown sugar with one and a half cups of blueberries and a tablespoon of butter in a saucepan. Simmer

this mixture for about five minutes. Grease a cake pan and pour the mixture in. Then add a cake batter. Here is one:

⅓ cup shortening	1¾ cups flour
1 cup sugar	¼ teaspoon salt
1 beaten egg	½ cup orange juice

Cream the shortening and sugar. Add the egg and beat very well. Add the sifted dry ingredients alternately with the orange juice. Then spoon it over the berry mixture, spreading evenly. Bake in a moderate oven twenty-five to forty minutes.

Can you imagine it served warm with whipped cream?

BLUEBERRY CAKE

Here is a thickly-berried cake recipe.

4 cups blueberries	4 cups sifted flour
¼ cup butter	4 teaspoons baking powder
1 cup sugar	2 cups milk
3 eggs	salt

Wash, dry and flour the berries. Cream the butter and sugar. Beat the eggs and add them to the sugar and butter. Then add the sifted flour, salt and baking powder alternately with the milk. Stir in the berries and bake in a large pan for thirty minutes at about 350 degrees.

BLUEBERRY PIE

2 eggs	2 teaspoons vanilla
1 cup granulated sugar	2 tablespoons powdered
2 cups blueberries	sugar
1 cup light cream	1 tablespoon lemon juice
1 teaspoon salt	1 unbaked pie crust
2 tablespoons flour	

Beat the egg yolks till light yellow. Add the sugar and beat again. Add the blueberries, cream, vanilla, salt, powdered sugar, lemon juice and flour. Pour this into the pastry-lined pie plate and bake at 425 degrees for ten minutes, then for another twenty-five minutes at 350 degrees.

For a simpler recipe: Mix four cups of blueberries with a quarter cup of flour and one cup of sugar. Sprinkle with lemon juice and a dusting of cinnamon. Pile into a pastry-lined pie tin. Add a top crust or criss-cross.

BLUEBERRY JAM

1½ quarts berries   *7 cups sugar*
juice of half a lemon   *¼ teaspoon cinnamon*
grated ½ lemon rind   *¼ teaspoon allspice*

Boil together rapidly for five minutes. Bottle and seal.

You can begin to look for blueberries towards the end of July, and you will find that they go on for almost a month. Picking blueberries is a joy. They are not brambly like raspberries and blackberries, nor as low to the ground as strawberries. They very often grow in crevices on otherwise bare rock, so they are easy to get at. And they are perfectly beautiful, presenting clumps of round plump dusty blueberries for the picking.

On a canoe trip in Temagami we had in blueberries a constant source of fresh fruit, a welcome change from the dried fruit we carried with us. Here is a dessert I made from half a package of pudding mix, which was all we had left.

I made up the mix (it was butterscotch), using a little more milk than was called for. The minute it was bubbly and cooked, but not thick, I took it off the heat and dumped in a heaping cup of blueberries.

The result was marvellous. The berries did not actually cook, but they plumped out, and when you ate them they burst in your mouth and spurted their juice out. The pudding was almost like a sauce, and could be used as such on plain cake or ice-cream. Thickened, it would make a delicious pie filling.

CANOE-TRIP PANCAKES

1 cup pancake or tea-
biscuit mix
1 powdered egg
1½ cups of water

powdered milk, in the
proportion necessary
for the water
1 heaping cup of blue-
berries

Stir together the pancake mix, the powdered egg and the powdered milk. Add the water, beating until you have a runny batter. Then add the berries. Drop by spoonfuls on to the frying pan, tipping the pan to let the batter spread. Flip when the pancakes are brown.

These make lovely thin pancakes, juicy with berries, and about twelve (small ones) in number. They are excellent to carry with you as a lunch snack, to be eaten cold.

Saskatoons

The saskatoon is a berry of the West which grows thickly on tall bushes, especially along the river banks and in the coulees. Expatriates of the Prairies, misty-eyed with memories, have told me of glorious picnic afternoons devoted to filling tin pails with the large reddish-brown berries.

You can use saskatoons, like blueberries, in many ways: you can eat them raw with sugar and cream, preserve them,

make jam and jelly from them, muffins and pancakes. Or, if you happen to have some dried bison meat around, you can mix them with it and make yourself some pemmican.

MRS. DARNELL'S SASKATOON PIE

3 *cups of saskatoons,*	*½ cup sugar*
washed	*¼ teaspoon nutmeg*
2 *tablespoons flour*	*(optional)*
2 *tablespoons lemon juice* or	*½ cup chopped rhubarb*

Line a nine-inch pie plate with pastry. Mix sugar, flour and nutmeg. Sprinkle some in the bottom of the pie, add the saskatoons, and then the remaining ingredients. Cover with a top crust and seal the edges. Bake at 450 degrees for fifteen minutes and then at 350 for about twenty-five minutes more.

Wild cherries

> "Of wild cherries there are many different species, but they are more medicinal than palatable; steeped in whiskey, with syrup added, the black cherry is used as a flavour for cordials; and the inner bark made into an extract, is given for agues and intermittents, and also in chest diseases."
> Mrs. C. P. Traill: *Female Emigrant's Guide* (1854)

Nevertheless, the wild cherry makes into a delicious jelly. The species vary in colour from purple black to the bright red of the smaller pincherry. You will find cherry trees growing along the sides of lanes and back roads, the fruit ripening in late August.

cherries, enough to   *2 pounds sugar*
  make 3 cups of juice   *1 bottle commercial pectin*

You will need a large paperbagful of cherries, or, to be more exact, about three quarts, to make the above amount of juice. Add to the fruit three cups of water, bring to a boil and simmer for fifteen minutes. Then squeeze out in a jelly-bag.

Now take the liquid, put into a preserving kettle and mix the sugar well into it. Bring it to a boil, stirring all the time. Now stir in the pectin, after which bring to a full rolling boil for one minute, stirring.

Remove from heat and bottle.

Strawberries

Once in a Paris restaurant a little brown wicker basket was brought to us, a layer of fresh green leaves turned back to reveal the rosy gleam of small perfectly-shaped wild strawberries, picked in the country that morning. Would we care to have them for dessert?

We would and did. Wild strawberries, with a plate of cream, whipped! I truly believe there is no sweeter, more delectable dessert.

How anyone picked them so carefully without squashing them I cannot imagine. However, the smell of squashed strawberries under a hot sun is part of the pleasure of picking them. Wild strawberries are usually ripe by the end of June or in early July. You will find them, close to the ground of course, in the woods, in meadows, on the sloping banks of country roads, and in gravelly areas.

Dr. William Butler remarked that doubtless God could have made a better berry, but doubtless He never did.

WILD STRAWBERRY SOUP

Fruit soups are most refreshing – and simple to prepare – for a hot summer's day. This soup requires a cucumber, some berries and some peanuts.

Grate the cucumber (just a small one or half a large one); mash the berries (½ to 1 cup) and chop or flake a couple of tablespoons of peanuts. Mix them together and serve, preferably with a generous dollop of sour cream.

POLISH STRAWBERRY SOUP

1 pound hulled washed   *5 dessertspoons cream*
   berries (about 1 pint)   *1½ pints water*
4 dessertspoons sugar

Crush the strawberries with the sugar. Add the water, cold, and then add the cream. Stir thoroughly. It is now ready to serve with hot biscuits or brown rolls.

SALAD

Lucy Yates in *The Gardener and the Cook*, says "A salad of fresh strawberries we dress in Italian fashion – that is, with sugar and the juice of lemons. To our thinking this is nicer and certainly more refreshing than thick cream can be, and it gives more value to the flavour of the fruit."

On the other hand, the Spanish method is to moisten the strawberries with sweet orange juice, which is very pleasant too.

I think most of us in this country do not go in for fresh fruit salads as much as we should and could. In summer such a salad could provide the entire lunch.

Take a large bowl and such fruits as the following: a fresh pineapple cut up in very tiny dices; a honeydew melon cut out into little balls; some oranges peeled most carefully and sliced and seeded; and finally as many wild strawberries as you like. Serve this with whatever dressing you think fit, but I should like to suggest this one:

Half a cup honey, one cup mayonnaise, a quarter-cup orange juice. Beat these ingredients and serve in a dish.

DESSERTS

Cardinal Wolsey, gastronomic fellow-roisterer of Henry VIII, is said to be the genius who first put cream to strawberries.

I would say that you cannot improve on strawberries and cream. Perhaps even that is too fancy. You cannot really improve on wild strawberries without cream, with only warmth and sunshine and approximately two seconds in time between their being plucked and being eaten. Then come wild strawberries and cream. So any recipes for other desserts cannot be considered improvements; they are merely departures from the natural state.

STRAWBERRIES & WHIPPED CREAM

Whip a cup of cream, sugar to taste with icing sugar, and mix in with as many wild berries as you wish. Heap in tall goblets to serve. To be very elegant, add half a cup of Kirsch to the berries.

Or, buy or bake an angel cake. Spread the cream and berry mixture over the top and into the hole and, if some is left over, down the sides of the cake. A banana or two cut up with the berries makes a pleasant addition.

Wild fruits   11

WILD STRAWBERRY ICE BOX CAKE

2 envelopes gelatine
½ cup cold water
1 cup mashed wild
  berries
1 cup sugar
2 dozen lady fingers

1 to 2 cups sweetened
  whipping cream (depend-
  ing on how reckless,
  monetarily and dieteti-
  cally, you feel)
1 teaspoon vanilla or
  Cointreau
1 cup whole berries

Soak the gelatine in cold water for five minutes. Set over boiling water to dissolve. Heat the mashed berries with the sugar until the sugar dissolves. Add the gelatine, and stir. Let it cool.

Split the lady fingers and line the bottom and sides of a pan or bowl. Whip the cream stiff, flavour it with vanilla or Cointreau and fold gently into the gelatine mixture. Blend it well and fold in the whole berries. Then pour the mixture into the lady-fingered bowl. Chill until firm. When ready to serve, unmold it and decorate it with sweetened whipped cream and the odd berry if you have any left over.

WILD STRAWBERRY ICE

1 quart or thereabouts
  of strawberries

½ cup sugar

Put the fruit through a sieve and mix it with the sugar. Then mash it all through the sieve again. Put in the freezer and freeze, but not too terribly hard. This is very pleasant and beautifully flavourful. It melts quickly and is especially nice in the melty stage.

WILD STRAWBERRY ICE CREAM (1)

1 quart berries
2 cups sugar

½ pint thick cream
1 pint milk

Put the fruit through a colander or strainer. Mix with it the sugar, cream, and milk, and pour into the freezing tray to freeze.

WILD STRAWBERRY ICE CREAM (2)

1 cup of wild berries
  mashed a bit
2 tablespoons corn
  syrup
pinch of salt

⅔ cup fine sugar
½ pint whipping cream,
  whipped
1 tablespoon lemon juice

Mix all but the cream together, stirring well to dissolve the sugar. Very gradually fold the berry mixture into the whipped cream. Turn into a refrigerator tray and freeze.

STRAWBERRY SHORTCAKE

Of course one may use all kinds of fruit for shortcakes. Blueberry shortcake is not nearly as popular as strawberry shortcake but it makes a delicious dessert. Here is the shortcake part of the recipe:

3 cups sifted flour
3 teaspoons baking
  powder
1 tablespoon sugar

½ teaspoon salt
5 tablespoons butter
1 egg, well beaten
⅔ to ¾ cup milk

Sift together the flour, baking powder, sugar and salt. Cut in the butter until the mixture is like cornmeal. Combine two-thirds of a cup of milk with the beaten egg, and add to the above mixture. Stir only until it is thoroughly moistened. If it appears to be too rough and stiff, add a little more milk. Grease a pan and bake in a hot oven fifteen to twenty minutes or until it seems to be done.

Of course it should be served warm. Split it in half (this I find a tricky business, but it's all right if it crumbles a bit, you can stick it together again). Then, you can butter it if you like, though that is pure swank. Crush some of the wild berries and place them on the bottom half. Replace the top half and pile on the whole berries. Then smother it all with as much whipped cream as you think good for you.

WILD STRAWBERRY WHIP

*1 cup berries – smashed
  and pulpy ones are fine*
⅛ teaspoon salt

½ cup sugar
2 egg whites, beaten stiffly
1 tablespoon lemon juice

Heat the berries, salt and sugar until the sugar is dissolved. Pour this hot syrup slowly over the beaten egg whites, beating constantly. Add the lemon juice and pile in parfait glasses. Serve immediately. As usual, cream may be added without spoiling anything.

WILD STRAWBERRY DROPS

½ pound icing sugar
*½ pint wild crushed
  berries*

*2 whites of eggs, stiffly
  beaten*

Mix the icing sugar into the whipped egg whites, add the crushed berries, and drop by the spoonful in cake tins or on waxed paper on a cookie sheet. Bake in an oven which is cooling (no more than 200 degrees).

STRAWBERRY PIE

In my opinion strawberries should never be left for hours soaking in sugar. It ruins the flavour and the texture, just as it does to bake them in a pie. I think the best strawberry pie consists

of a thin baked shell, into which the wild strawberries are put uncooked, sprinkled with brown or very fine sugar and served with whipped cream.

WILD STRAWBERRY JELLY

> 4 cups wild strawberry   7 cups sugar
>   juice   1 bottle pectin

To get your juice, crush the berries. I usually add about a half cupful of water. Place in a cheesecloth and squeeze into your kettle. Add the sugar, mix well, bring to a rolling boil, stirring constantly.

Stir in pectin, boil again for one minute. Remove from heat and pour.

Wild strawberry jam or jelly is delicious on brown bread with packaged cream cheese or cottage cheese.

WILD STRAWBERRY JAM

Gather one quart of wild strawberries. Cover them with boiling water, and let them stay in it for five minutes, no longer. Then drain them thoroughly. Now add to them one cup of sugar, put them on the stove and boil furiously for five minutes. Then add another cup plus a third more, of sugar. Bring again to the boil and boil hard for eight minutes.

Then remove the pan from the stove and the skim from the jam. After which stir the jam gently for a little over five minutes, before potting.

STRAWBERRY AND GOOSEBERRY JAM

> 3 pounds wild strawberries   3 pounds sugar
> 1½ pounds gooseberries
> (or red currants which also contain pectin)

Place the gooseberries in a saucepan with enough water to cover them. Simmer until they are mushy, and strain off the juice. Put your strawberries and this juice into a preserving kettle, bring to a boil and boil gently twenty-five to thirty minutes. Then stir in the sugar and, when it is dissolved, boil quickly for about ten minutes.

Test for setting by pouring some on a plate. If it is sticky and wrinkles when you push it after a few seconds, then it is ready. Pour into prepared jars.

There is one other use of the strawberry plant: it is said that a tisane of strawberry leaves is recommended for gravel in the bladder and the kidneys.

Gooseberries

"Gathered wild gooseberries, and when they were stewed found them excellent sauce for salmon."
The Diary of Mrs. John Graves Simcoe (1792-1795)

There are two kinds of wild gooseberry – the kind with prickles and the kind without. I mean, it is the berries themselves that are sometimes be-prickled, though they are no less edible than the smooth ones. And, in the compensatory way that nature sometimes has, the prickly ones seem to grow larger than the others, and to have a gloriously red leaf which is not only aesthetically satisfying, but a help in identification. The wild

gooseberry ripens around the second week of August, give and take a little both ways, which is before Autumn has taken the green from other plants. Thus, should you see a somewhat trailing, graceful strand of a plant with small red leaves, hanging down over rock, there is a good chance it is a gooseberry.

Wild gooseberries do not grow to the enormous size of tame ones, nor are they as plentiful as most other wild fruits.

WILD GOOSEBERRY TART

Somehow gooseberries seem to deserve, or require, a very flaky pastry. Consequently, I would suggest using a puff pastry for your tart, which rather enhances the appearance of the end product.

Bake your crust first, perhaps in individual tartlets if you prefer. Here is one recipe for it:

4 cups flour
1 tablespoon salt
1 tablespoon sugar

1 pound sweet butter
1¼ cups ice water

Mix the salt and sugar with the flour. With the fingers rub in one third of the butter. Add the ice water, stirring with a knife until you have a smooth dough. Flour a board sparingly. Roll the paste out carefully to quarter-inch thickness. Spread bits of butter on it. Sprinkle with flour. Then fold the pastry over, one third from each side, to meet in the middle. Then fold the ends over. Now roll it down again to about a third of an inch.

Then add the rest of the butter in bits and fold as before. Repeat the folding and rolling at least three times more. Then chill the dough for at least an hour.

If it should stick during the rolling process, rather than add more flour, chill the dough for short periods. Cook it in a hot oven.

Now, there are several ways of proceeding. You can put your berries, raw, into the cooked shell and *heavily* coat them with sugar. Then the tart may be nicely completed with a layer of sweetened whipped cream.

However, I really think in the case of wild gooseberries it is better to cook them first. Stew them and add plenty of sugar when they are cooked. Then lay them in the freshly baked puff pastry crust, and serve with plenty of thick cream, or a custard.

Or, lay the raw berries in uncooked puff paste, add sugar, cover with a top crust and bake in the oven fairly quickly, until done.

SIMPLY STEWED

gooseberries   *sugar*

You will need plenty of sugar, for they are tart little berries. I suggest one cup of sugar to two of berries. However, because you add the sugar after the berries have been cooked, you can add sugar to your own taste. When you have snipped off the ends of the gooseberries, wash them, put them in a saucepan without water but with a lid, and cook for five to ten minutes, or until they seem done. Then turn the heat off and add sugar.

GOOSEBERRY WHIP

2 cups gooseberries   *whites of 2 or 3 eggs*
1 cup sugar

Stew the fruit as in the recipe for stewed gooseberries. Then fold them into the very stiffly beaten whites of two or three eggs.

Gooseberries are so very sour, even with sugar, that they are really best served with something else to tone them down – for instance the smooth blandness of a custard, or the shortness of pastry.

18   *Gooseberries*

GOOSEBERRY FOOL

This is a dish composed of custard and stewed berries.

2 cups gooseberries
1 cup granulated
  sugar
3 eggs

1 pint milk
cinnamon
icing sugar

Stew gooseberries with sugar and when well done put them through a not too fine sieve, or leave them as they are. Now beat the eggs very well. Mix them into a pint of milk and put the mixture into the top part of a double boiler. Add a little cinnamon and cook over boiling water.

When it has come to the boiling point remove and let cool. Sweeten with icing sugar and gradually add the gooseberries or the gooseberry pulp.

Or if you have any custard powder in the house you can use that, rather than make your own custard.

WILD GOOSEBERRY JAM

Take gooseberries and sugar, half as much of the latter as the former. Gooseberries are rich in pectin so that if you cook the two ingredients together for about half an hour, you should have a jam that sets.

ANOTHER RECIPE FOR JAM

3 pounds gooseberries
2 cups water

3 pounds sugar

Boil the fruit with the water for fifteen minutes. Remove from heat and add the sugar, stirring until dissolved. Then bring to the boil and continue boiling rapidly until set. This will probably take about twenty minutes. (Test by putting a few drops on a cold saucer. Blow lightly, and if the liquid wrinkles and appears sticky, it is ready.)

Cranberries

After the strawberries and raspberries and blueberries, in fact just before the Autumn frosts, come the cranberries. You will find them during September, round orange-red globes glowing amongst the moss and their own shiny green leaves, in slight hollows of rocky terrain. Many of them grow, if not in actual boggy areas, at least amongst squishy moss. Once you have found some good patches you can fill a six-quart basket easily.

The most usual thing to do with them is to make cranberry sauce or cranberry jelly, the traditional accompaniment to Thanksgiving turkey. Cranberry sauce "makes rich open tarts" says Mrs. Traill in *Female Emigrant's Guide* "or can be served ... to eat with bread."

CRANBERRY SAUCE

1 pint berries   *1 pound sugar*
1 pint water

Wash and drain the cranberries. Stew them in the water until the skins burst, then add the sugar and bring them all to a boil. Boil gently for half an hour, then empty into a bowl or mould.

CRANBERRY JELLY

2 quarts or so of cranberries   *7 cups of sugar*
  to make 5 cups of juice

Crush the cranberries, add three cups of water, put in a sauce-pan and bring to the boil. Simmer for ten minutes, covered. Then squeeze out the juice. Add the sugar and mix well with the juice. Put this into a saucepan, place over heat and bring to a boil. Boil for fifteen minutes and then bottle.

When you feel you have bottled all the sauce and jelly you could want, here are a few other ways of using cranberries:

CRANBERRY SOUP

This is for (a) those who are vegetarians and (b) those who do not believe in cooking their food.
  Chop up one cup of cranberries and press the juice out with a potato masher or something equally effective. Flake half a cup of peanuts and put them in the juice. Add two cups of tepid water and a teaspoon of honey. Beat well and serve.

CRANBERRY NUT LOAF

2 cups jellied cranberry   *¼ cup powdered sugar*
  sauce   *1 teaspoon vanilla*
¾ cup grated and peeled   *½ cup chopped walnuts or*
  apple   *pecans*
½ pint of cream, whipped

Crush the sauce with a fork and stir in the apple. Pour it into a refrigerator tray. Then combine the whipped cream with the sugar, vanilla, and a third of the nuts. Layer this over the fruit mixture. Sprinkle the remaining nuts over the top, and freeze until firm. This is a very pleasant dessert. I would suggest you take it out of the freezing compartment half an hour before serving, and put it in another part of the refrigerator.

RAW CRANBERRY SALAD

2 cups raw cranberries   1 package lemon gelatine
1 orange, peeled   1 cup boiling water
1 cup sugar   ¼ cup chopped walnuts
                        (optional)

Wash the berries and put them through a grinder. Then grind the orange and add it to the cranberries. Add the sugar and the nuts. Dissolve the lemon gelatine in boiling water, then chill. When slightly thick, fold in the cranberry and orange mixture. Pour into moulds and chill until firm.

CRANBERRY RELISH

1 quart cranberries   1 cup unsalted nuts
1 large orange   ¾ cup brown sugar
1 large apple

Grind everything up, leaving the orange and apple unpeeled (but of course remove seeds and core). Add the sugar and chill before serving.

CRANBERRY ICE

To a pot of cranberry jelly, add the juice of half a lemon and a tablespoon of orange juice. Whip half a pint of cream and fold into the softened jelly. Freeze.

CRANBERRY DESSERT

4 cups cranberries   juice of 1 lemon
2 cups sugar   1 tablespoon grated
                        orange rind

Cook the cranberries with a quarter cup of water until the skins pop. Combine the hot cranberry mush with the other ingre-

dients and stir well to dissolve the sugar. Cool. Then chill and freeze.

Here is an old Canadian recipe:

CRANBERRY TARTS

Stewed, strained and sweetened, put into paste No. 9. Add spices till grateful and bake gently.

and Paste No. 9 is called Royal Paste.

Rub half a pound of butter into one pound of flour, four whites beat to a foam, two ounces fine sugar; roll often, rubbing one third, and rolling two thirds of butter is best; excellent for tarts.

CRANBERRY MUFFINS

2½ cups flour
4 teaspoons baking
   powder
1½ teaspoons salt
¼ cup sugar

1 cup fresh cranberries,
   chopped fine
1 teaspoon grated orange rind
½ cup shortening
1 egg, beaten
1 cup milk

Stir flour, baking powder, salt, sugar, and orange rind in a bowl. Cut in shortening. Add egg and milk, and mix well together. Fold in the cranberries. Bake in greased muffin pans at 425 degrees for twenty-five to thirty minutes.

SPICED CRANBERRIES – to serve over meats

4 cups brown sugar
1¼ cups vinegar
1 teaspoon cinnamon
1 teaspoon allspice

1 teaspoon ground cloves
½ teaspoon ground ginger
3 pounds cranberries

Boil sugar, vinegar and spices for twenty minutes. Add the cranberries and boil slowly for two hours.

Put a teacup of cranberries into a cup of water, mash. Boil two quarts water with one tablespoon of oatmeal and a bit of lemon-peel. Add berries and as much fine sugar as shall leave a smart flavour of the fruit, and a quarter pint sherry. Boil half an hour, strain.

H. I. Richards: *Canadian Housewife's Manual of Cookery* (1861)

Wild plums

> "Among our wild fruits we have plums which, in some townships, are very fine and abundant; these make admirable preserves, especially when boiled in maple molasses."
> Mrs. C. P. Traill: *The Backwoods of Canada* (1836)

Wild plums ripen towards the middle of September – when wild cherries and chokecherries are fullest and ripest. It is a delight to find a wild plum tree, for they are by no means plentiful. I believe there are two kinds. One produces a small oval-round red fruit about the size of an alley. The other wild plum is slightly larger and more purple. They are both delicious to eat raw (but only when fully ripe). They also make jelly; stew deliciously; and may be brandied.

WILD PLUM JELLY

Wash the plums, put them in a large saucepan and cover them – just – with water. Let them boil until very tender – probably twenty minutes to half an hour.

When they are ready, let the juice strain through a fine sieve or jelly bag. Be sure to measure the juice, and remember how many cups you have. Return it to the saucepan and boil. Now measure the sugar, in a quantity equal to the amount of juice you started with, and set it in an oven dish in a warm oven. When the juice has boiled twenty-five minutes, add the hot sugar, stirring well. Bring the whole to a boil, boil for one minute, and then pour into prepared jars.

STEWED WILD PLUMS

2 pounds plums *⅓ cup water*
2½ cups sugar

Rinse and drain the plums well, making sure they are all good specimens. Boil the sugar and water. If you feel you have too little water, add a quarter-cup more. Boil until the syrup is clear and then add the plums. Boil for two minutes. They will have a thick rich juice, and will be even better the second day.

WILD PLUMS IN BRANDY

Use the same amounts of plums, sugar and water as for stewing (doubling the amounts if you wish, and can). In addition, you will need one cup of brandy (doubling that also if you double the other amounts).

When you have washed the plums, take a needle, dip it in boiling water, and then prick each plum around where the stem joins the plum.

Proceed to make the syrup as for stewing. When clear, drop in the plums, boil them for two minutes, and remove to a china or pyrex or stone dish. Cover them very tightly (fruit flies are in great abundance at this time of year and multiply mysteriously if you have any fruit around). Let them sit twenty-four to forty-eight hours.

You will probably find that many of the skins have come off, and more will come off as you take your next step. I would suggest you leave them with the plums anyway.

Pour off all the syrup into a saucepan, place it over the fire and boil for half an hour, or until it forms a soft ball in cold water.

Then take it off the fire, add the brandy, put the plums into sterilized jars and *fill to the very top* with the brandy-and-syrup. Cover at once. It is well to let them sit for three months.

This is a truly divine way of preparing a divine little plum. And you will feel equally celestial after taking a dish of them.

Chokecherries

Chokecherries are the most luscious looking fruit imaginable. Who has not been tempted to eat an entire cluster of the rich round translucent berries? The result of yielding to such a temptation is quite dreadful, for they pucker up the mouth like ten dozen dry soda biscuits. But they make a lovely jelly, rather sweet.

CHOKECHERRY JELLY

chokecherries   *sugar*
water

Add half a cup of water to every cup of fruit. Boil it and simmer for at least fifteen minutes. Then crush the fruit with a heavy glass or some such thing, after which strain the juice. (I do a preliminary strain through the sieve, *then* use the cheesecloth.) Now, for every cup of juice, use two and a quarter cups of sugar. Boil the two together for twenty minutes. Then test it by putting half a spoonful on a plate and watching to see if it thickens. It may need half to three quarters of an hour to boil, as cherries are not terribly rich in pectin.

CHERRYWHIP SAUCE

water
chokecherries

sugar
egg whites

Make some cherry syrup by putting half a cup of water to every cup of chokecherries. Boil twenty minutes and mash through a sieve. Add sugar, twice as many cups as there are of juice, and boil about twenty-five minutes. At that time, whip two egg whites stiff.

Now, turn up the heat beneath the juice until it is a pink froth. Snatch it off the stove just before it spills over, and slowly dribble spoonfuls into the egg white, beating at the same time. (It helps to have someone else do the dribbling.) Gradually you will find it turns a beautiful pale pinky-mauve shade. You may stop when the colour suits you, and you have a gorgeous light sauce for a pudding.

CHOKECHERRY WINE

There are two things to remember when making chokecherry wine. One is, never boil the chokecherries to extract the juice, because the milky emulsion which results will not make a wine. The other is, taste the wine at its various stages – you can improve it to your own satisfaction as you go along.

Apart from the ingredients, you will need a receptacle for the wine while it is working, and bottles for when it is ready. If you have a corking machine, then you could save old wine bottles and fit them with new corks. Otherwise, I suggest that you use any bottles with screw tops. For the receptacle, you use a wooden cask or a gallon vinegar jar with a thermos flask cork. Bore a hole through the middle of the cork and insert a piece of rubber tubing 18 inches to 2 feet long. Then have some melted wax on hand.

chokecherries　　　　　　*toast*
sugar　　　　　　　　　*brewers' yeast*

28　　　*Wild grapes*

First, gather the chokecherries, as many as you please. Put them into a large kettle or tub and crush them. The easiest way is to tread them with your feet. Then strain them, keeping the juice and throwing away the skins and stalks. Add three pounds of sugar to each gallon of juice. Put the juice into the cask or the gallon jar (or jars), filling them to within two inches of the top.

Now, cut the toast into quarters, spread them with bakers' or brewers' yeast, and float them on top. Lightly bung the cask, or if you are using a jar, wax the whole of the cork so no air can get in, and put the free end of the tubing into a small jar of water. This is to allow gas to escape without letting air into the cask or jar. Otherwise you will finish up with vinegar.

It will now start fermenting. Leave it for three months, insuring that no air gets to the wine by tightening the bung of the cask after two weeks, or keeping the small jars filled with water.

Now comes the important process of bottling. Decant or siphon off the clear liquid, filling the bottles you are going to use. There will be a considerable amount of sediment left behind.

Cork the bottles well or, if you are using screw caps, tighten them firmly.

Leave the bottles lying on their side in a cool place for as long as you can. The reward will be greater if you leave the wine for a year or two.

Wild grapes

The small compact clusters of tiny purple wild grapes make a jelly that is both tart enough to accompany meats and sweet enough to spread on bread. One vine, tangling up a tree or

spreading along a fence, is likely to yield a sackful of grapes which will provision your shelves amply for a winter. The thick rich juice which you must first brew before you get your jelly makes an excellent basis for cold drinks while the warm weather yet remains. You can keep it, undiluted, in the refrigerator, simply adding water and ice to taste. Or you can fancy it up as you think fit.

WILD GRAPE JUICE AND JELLY

I leave the grapes in their bunches, washing them a sieveful at a time. Then I put them into a large kettle and crush them with a wooden spoon or a cup. Next, having added a cup or so of water, I bring it to a boil for about ten minutes, stirring a bit to help get the juice out. Then comes the somewhat tiresome process of squeezing out the juice through cheesecloth or a jelly-bag. You will need another good-sized saucepan or pail for this, and you mustn't mind that your fingers will get rather blue.

Measure out your juice. For every four cups of juice I think about six cups of sugar are sufficient, with the juice of one lemon. Put grape juice, sugar and lemon juice together and bring to the boil, stirring constantly.

Now, if you want some grape juice on hand, pour as much as you want into a jug or a milk bottle. Treat the milk bottle carefully, scalding it first (a) to clean it and (b) to prepare it for the hot liquid.

This is a rich delicious juice, and children will probably think up all sorts of concoctions to make with it, such as ice-cream sodas, made by adding ice-cream and soda water.

Now, boil the remainder again, and either stir in pectin according to the directions on the bottle, or keep boiling it for twenty minutes, then test it on a plate. If it wrinkles stickily when you blow on it, it is ready for bottling.

WILD GRAPE JELLY – another method

1 peck of wild grapes   *½ cup cinnamon*
1 quart vinegar   *12 cups sugar*
½ cup whole cloves

Bring the grapes, vinegar, cloves and cinnamon just to the boiling point, and strain. Then boil the resulting liquid for twenty minutes. Add twelve cups of sugar and boil until it tests for jelling, in about five minutes.

WILD GRAPE BUTTER

apples   *sugar*
grapes

For this, you need as many apples as grapes. Stew the apples and mash them; mash the grapes and add to the apples. Press the juice out as best you can (by now you may well be wishing for a fruit press, and I think it is a very worthwhile investment), add half as much sugar as there is pulp, and cook until thick. Be careful that it does not burn.

SPICED GRAPE SAUCE

Here is a further use for your grape juice. Combine:

>1 tablespoon cornstarch
>2 tablespoons sugar
>½ teaspoon cinnamon
>1 cup of your grape juice

Bring these to a boiling point and cook gently until thickened. Remove from heat and add:

>1 tablespoon lemon juice
>1 tablespoon margarine or butter

The sauce is now ready to be used on desserts.

Elderberries

The elderberry ripens towards the end of summer and the beginning of autumn. There are red elderberries and black or deep purple ones – and it is only the purple elderberries which are edible. The berries are borne on a compound cyme looking like an umbrella that is all ribs and no material, each rib having a tiny rounded end which is a berry.

ELDERBERRY JAM

The preliminary de-stalking of the elderberries is more onerous than that of most other fruits. I would suggest that you clean and stalk them at a time when there is a good radio program on.

>1 pound elderberries (about 2 cups)
>¾ pound sugar (1⅓ cups)
>2 teaspoons water

Having removed all the stems and washed the berries, add the sugar and water and cook until almost thick. Test at twenty minutes. Do not cook over half an hour. Bottle.

ELDERBERRY JAM – another method

> 6 pounds elderberries
> 4 pounds sugar
> 1 tablespoon orange flavouring

Boil the berries with a little water for fifteen minutes, having first weighed the fruit. To six pounds of berries allow four pounds of sugar. Add the sugar, boil another forty-five minutes, then add a tablespoon of orange flavour water. Bottle.

ELDERBERRY JELLY

> 5 quarts berries   5 pounds sugar
> juice of 2 lemons

Use about five quarts of ripe berries. Place in a saucepan and crush. Heat gently and simmer fifteen minutes. Then squeeze out the juice in a jelly bag. Put the juice (you should have about three cups) in a saucepan with the lemon juice. Add the sugar to the juice and mix well. Bring to a boil and boil gently for twenty minutes. Test on a plate. If a spoonful does not thicken in a few seconds, boil for another five minutes and test again. When it is ready, pour into jars and seal.

ELDERBERRY KETCHUP

> 2 cups elderberries   1 small piece ginger root
> 1½ cups boiling vinegar   30 white peppercorns
> ½ teaspoon salt   10 cloves
> 4 shallots   a grating of nutmeg

Strip the berries from the stalks, measure, pour boiling vinegar over them. Stand for one night. Next day strain off the liquor, boil five minutes with the spices. Bottle when cold.

ELDERBERRY CHUTNEY

This may be made in larger quantities. If you double the amount of berries, double everything else.

1 pound berries	*1 cup raisins*
1 onion	*pinch of cayenne*
8 cloves	*1 teaspoon salt*
½ teaspoon ginger	*pinch of mace*
¼ cup brown sugar	*½ teaspoon mustard seed*
1 cup vinegar	

Pound all together. Boil ten minutes. Remove, cover and leave until cold. Then bottle.

ELDERBERRY WINE

½ peck elderberries	*¼ teaspoon ground allspice*
1½ gallons boiling water	*1 lb. chopped raisins*
3 pounds sugar	*1 tablespoon brewers' yeast*
¼ ounce ginger	*or 1 cake compressed yeast*
4 cloves	*½ cup brandy*

Gather ripe berries, stalk them and crush them in a large crock. Pour over them the boiling water. Cover, leave 24 hours. Then put through sieve into a preserving pan and add sugar, spices and raisins. Simmer one hour, skimming. Let stand until only warm, pour into cask or gallon jars. Spread two or three-inch squares of toast with yeast and float them on top. Leave for two weeks or until it stops working. Add half a cup of brandy to each gallon. Bung the cask tightly now or, if using glass jars, pour

into sterilized bottles and cork or screw tops on tightly. The wine may be bottled (or rebottled) in four to six months' time.

MURIEL'S ELDERBERRY CRISP

2 cups elderberries	1 cup brown sugar
granulated sugar	½ cup butter
1 cup oatmeal	½ cup of flour

Put the cleaned, stemmed elderberries into the bottom of a casserole or other oven dish and sweeten to taste with white sugar. Then make the topping by combining the oatmeal, brown sugar, butter and flour. Sprinkle this over the berries, and bake until the crust is crisp and golden.

Raspberries

"Well-ripened raspberries and red currants mixed with a few tart cherries, what a delicious summer salad do they not make, especially if a suspicion of liquor lurks within the bowl. The only dressing they need, if you mix them early enough in the day, and set the bowl in a cool place for a few hours, is plenty of sugar and sufficient wine to moisten it, with that *goutte* of kummel or more delicate noyau."
    Lucy Yates: *The Gardener and the Cook* (1912)

Raspberry canes spring up in wild profusion around deserted farms, obliterating traces of man. They also grow along dirt roads, and as the season of ripening is high summer, you will want to wash your berries well to take the dust from them. It is also wise to spread them out on paper afterwards, not only

to dry but to let anything with six legs or more remove itself from the tiny hollow cups.

I prefer raspberries with running cream (though it be ever so thick) to whipped cream. Nor do they seem to me to require sugar. They are good for breakfast, lunch, tea and dinner. They have the sweetest, most delightful flavour in the world and the only thing which keeps them from perfection is their rather extra-large seeds.

The black raspberry is often found growing side by side with the red raspberry. It too is delicious when fully ripe, but rather harder to pick because the core does not come out easily. The black raspberry is most suitable for jelly, and fortunately you will not need to remove its core when picking it for that purpose.

RASPBERRY SOUP

    4 cups raspberries   *sour cream*
    1 quart cold water

Cook four cups of raspberries in a quart of cold water until soft. Then pass them through a sieve. Sweeten this resulting purée to taste. Cool, and serve with ice or sour cream floating in it.

You may use a combination of raspberries and strawberries or any other berry ripe at the time.

DESSERTS

Raspberry Ice and Raspberry Shortcake may be made as for Strawberries, substituting the one fruit for the other.

RASPBERRY BAVARIAN CREAM

1 quart raspberries   *½ cup cold water*
1 cup sugar   *½ cup boiling water*
2 tablespoons gelatine   *1 pint whipping cream*

Mash the raspberries with the sugar, and let stand for one hour. Soak the gelatine in the cold water for the same length of time. Strain the juice from the berries, pressing them through the sieve.

Pour the hot water on the gelatine and dissolve it. Add the berry juice. Whip the cream and stir it into the juice mixture. Turn into a mould and chill. Serve with whipped cream.

RASPBERRY FLUFF

Take a good amount of raspberries, say a quart, or a small pailful. Whip one cup of whipping cream partially, then add the berries and keep whipping until the cream becomes pink from the berries and the whole thing is of a pleasant consistency. You may find a tablespoon or so of icing sugar is necessary. Then serve, preferably in glass dishes or goblets (purely for looks).

RASPBERRY TRIFLE

Trifle is really a glorified name for custard, cake and, traditionally, jam. In this case, we use fresh raspberries.

sponge cake or any left-
over cake cut into thin
slices
1 pint of custard

1 pint or more of fresh
ripe raspberries
sugar
whipping cream
tiny glass of sherry

If you have a glass fruit bowl it adds to the eye's pleasure if you use it for the trifle.

Line the bowl with the cake and, if you like, sprinkle the cake with sherry. Make your custard using a custard powder, if you are happy with it. Put the berries in, sprinkle them with sugar and pour the hot custard over them.

Smother it or dot it with whipped cream when the custard is cool enough that the cream does not melt and decorate it with candied violets if you have some.

RASPBERRY TARTS WITH CREAM

Roll out some thin puff paste and lay in a pan of what size you choose; put in raspberries, strew over them fine sugar, cover with a thin lid, then bake, cut it open and have ready the following mixture: warm half a pint of cream, the yolks of two or three eggs well beaten, and a little sugar and when this is added to the tarts return the whole to the oven for five or six minutes.

James Macfarlane: *The Cook Not Mad* (1831)

RASPBERRY CREAM

Make a quart of rich boiled custard. (See directions for Gooseberry Fool.) When cold pour it on a quart of ripe red raspberries; mash them in it, pass through a sieve, sweeten and freeze.

JAMS AND JELLIES

Here is an easy recipe for jam, though the result is rather crunchy and seedy.

3 *pounds raspberries*   3 *pounds sugar*

Place the fruit in a pan in a warm oven for a few minutes to heat through. Put the sugar in a separate pan and do the same with it. Mash the fruit a bit while it is heating, with a wooden spoon. When it is hot and well mashed, add the sugar. Stir it well until the sugar is dissolved, then boil it fast for six minutes.

RASPBERRY JELLY

Raspberry jelly brings out all the fragrant sweet flavour of the berries. It is not a jelly to eat with meats but rather with cream cheese, in sandwiches, or with Devonshire cream (if you can get it!) or cottage cheese on hot biscuits. Children may like it stirred into yoghurt or sour cream for dessert.

raspberries   *sugar*

Crush the berries and press out the juice. To assist the process, you might heat them *very* gently with half a cup of water for half an hour.

For each quart of juice obtained allow one and a half pounds of sugar. Add the sugar to the juice and boil for twenty to twenty-five minutes, making the usual test before bottling.

BEVERAGES

RASPBERRY CORDIAL

1 *quart raspberries*   *fruit sugar*
1 *quart brandy*

To each quart of berries add one quart of brandy. (You must be feeling affluent to make this cordial.) Let it stand for a week before straining it. Now, taste it and reduce the strength if you so desire, with water. If you have a gallon of beverage, add one pound of fruit sugar. Let it stand for a few weeks.

This beverage is considered to be "of singular efficacy in complaints of the chest". I should think so.

RASPBERRY VINEGAR

> 4 quarts raspberries   sugar
> vinegar

Into an earthenware jar put the raspberries and cover with vinegar. Let stand for twenty-four hours. Then bring it to the boil, just, strain it and add one pound of sugar to each pint of liquid. Boil the result for twenty minutes and bottle.

A large spoonful in a glass of water is said to be relished by the sick.

RASPBERRY WINE

> raspberries, gathered   sugar
>   when fully ripe   water

Bruise your berries, add an equal quantity of water, stir well and let the whole stand for two entire days, covered. Then strain through a fine sieve or cheesecloth bag, without forcing the juice through. Add six cups of sugar to every gallon of liquid. Then put it into a wooden cask or an earthenware crock or, if you don't possess either of these receptacles, into glass jars. It will be ready for bottling in about two months.

Rose hips

It is a joy to find in midsummer a dusty road edged with masses of wild pink roses. To know that this plant is useful as well as charming is an added bonus.

When the blossoms have long since fallen, around the beginning of September, the rose hips – that is, the fruit – become red and plump and ripe for picking.

ROSE HIP JELLY

Gather a bagful of hips, wash and dry them. Cut them in halves, lengthwise. Put them into a preserving kettle with a small amount of water. Cover and cook until tender, watching to see that they do not burn. Add a little more water if necessary.

Strain through a jelly-bag.

Measure the liquid and boil it for ten minutes. Then add one pound of sugar to each pint of juice you have, and boil until it jells well when a spoonful is put on a plate. Then bottle.

A small glass of wild rose hip jelly is a thoughtful and unusual gift.

Crabapples

Crabapples are, of course, those dear little babies' fists of apples which look so sweet and taste so horrid. But they do make a lovely jelly, delicately coloured and flavoured, a perfect accompaniment to ham.

CRABAPPLE JELLY WITH ROSE GERANIUM

Pick a nice large bag of crabapples. Wash them and cut them into small pieces, but don't bother to peel or core them. Add about a pint of water, or up to a quart if you have a great number of apples. Bring them to a boil and simmer ten to fifteen minutes. Crush them and continue simmering a few minutes, then strain them. The jelly will be clear and translucent if you let it drip by itself overnight without any help from you. However, if you are impatient, you may squeeze the juice out right away. The final appearance of the jelly will be rather cloudy, but the flavour is not affected.

Measure out your juice in cupfuls, into a large saucepan. For every cup of juice, put one half cup of sugar. Boil it for about fifteen minutes. Then test, and keep boiling it until the drops on the plate become stiff in a few seconds.

Pluck some leaves from a rose (or sweet) geranium plant, and wipe them. Place a leaf in the bottom of a jar, pour in the jelly, and wait until the leaf rises to the surface. Take it out, and seal the jar. Then put another leaf into another bottle and continue the process. If you like, you may leave the leaf *in* the jelly. I think the flavour is enhanced if you do, and it is easy to fish the leaf out when you open the pot of jelly, for it will be right at the top.

CRABAPPLE AND CRANBERRY JELLY

These two fruits are in season together, well on into September. Use about one quarter as many cranberries as crabapples.

Just cover your crabapples with water, cook for about 25 minutes, and then add the cranberries. Cover. When all is soft, turn into a jelly-bag and drip overnight. The trouble with the overnight dripping is that you are all keyed up to jelly-making and it is rather a let down to have to leave things halfway. You just have to make up your mind whether you want a clear jelly or not. Anyway, suppose you have let it drip during the night. You wake up in the morning to find all the lovely juice. Immediately (after getting breakfast for all and sundry and disposing of the family and the dishes) measure the amount of juice into a preserving kettle. Bring it to a boil and boil 20 minutes. Add sugar in an amount equal to the amount of the juice, and stir until it is dissolved. Boil well for five minutes and then bottle.

PRESERVED CRABAPPLES

Some crabapples are very crabbed and some are round and rosy and perfect. The crabbed ones can go into the jelly; for preserving, use the best ones you can find.

Leave the apples whole, but pare them and dig out the flower-buds. Make a syrup of twice as much sugar as water (six cups of sugar to three of water if you have a goodly number of apples, say, six to eight quarts). After boiling the syrup for five minutes, add the apples and cook slowly until they are tender – about half an hour. Then lift them out into sealers. Thicken the syrup a little by cooking it some more. Pour it over the crabapples, filling the bottles, and seal.

Wash and dry the fruit and make a syrup of the following:

1 pint cider vinegar   *1 bag of apples*
3 cups of brown sugar   *(say 6 quarts)*

Then assemble various spices such as cassia buds, a cinnamon stick broken up, cloves and allspice and a little ginger. Put these into a piece of muslin and tie it up. Then put it into the syrup and add as many crabapples as the vinegar syrup will cover. Cook slowly for half an hour or until tender. Pour into jars and seal.

May apples

May apples grow near the edge of open woods or along fences, looking like droopy green umbrellas, gnome-sized. The fruit, which has the appearance of a yellow plum, ripens at the end of July and the beginning of August. It is not prolific and you may have to search for some time before finding a patch of it. Perhaps this is the reason that the may apple is so little known or utilized.

The may apple can be eaten raw when fully ripe, or may be made into a jelly. Also, from the juice of the fruit can be obtained a beverage. For both juice and jelly, proceed along the same lines as for grape juice and jelly. But here is a recipe for something a little different.

MAY APPLE PRESERVE

This is well worth a try and very useful to have on hand as a surprise dessert for unexpected visitors.

> Gather the fruit as soon as it begins to shew any yellow tint on the green rind: lay them in a sunny window for a day or two; cut them in quarters and throw them into a syrup of white sugar in which ginger sliced, and cloves, have been boiled: boil the fruit till the outer rind is tender: take the fruit out and lay them in a basin, sift a handful of pounded sugar over them and let them lie till cold. Next day boil your syrup a second time, pour it over the fruit, and when cold put it into jars or glasses, and tie down. It should not be used till a month or six weeks after making.
>
> Mrs. C. P. Traill: *The Female Emigrant's Guide*
> (Toronto: 1854) p. 91

MAY APPLE MARMALADE

Collect your may apples – you will be fortunate to get a medium-sized bagful. Wash them and remove the skins, keeping them. Now put the skins into a saucepan and add a cup of water; bring to a boil and simmer for fifteen minutes, covered. Then add the pulp and simmer for another ten minutes. Measure.

Add twice as much sugar as you have fruit. Mix fruit and sugar together, bring to a boil, and boil until it passes the jelling test.

CHAPTER 2

Wild flowers

elderberry

dandelion

violet

Violets

The idea of nibbling on a violet or a rose petal savours of a Cleopatran luxury on a par with drinking pearls. To some people the idea is not a pleasant one, as though it were a wicked waste of beauty. This is nonsense, of course, since eating them is doing anything but wasting them.

Quite interesting things can be done with flowers, and we find that violets, made into a syrup, used to be (and who knows, may still be?) a cure for rheumatism of the right wrist. The specificity of the locale delights me – what, do you suppose, is good for rheumatism of the *left* wrist?

In case you are afflicted with the complaint, here is the recipe:

VIOLET SYRUP

Pour two and a half pints of boiling water over a pound of flowers (it will take some time to gather that many as they are very light indeed). Leave twenty-four hours, then pour the liquid off and strain. The strained liquid is made into syrup without boiling, by the addition of sugar, twice the quantity of the liquid.

CANDIED VIOLETS

sugar   *rosewater, or almond essence*
water   *violets*

Make a syrup of sugar and water (not much water – about a quarter cup to one cup of sugar) and boil for a while, stirring if it gets uppity. Add a little almond essence or rosewater and let the syrup cool. Now take the violets which you have gathered and which you have not allowed to dry out, and put some of them, a few at a time, into the syrup. Let them stay there for a minute or so, being sure they are treated all over, then remove them to wax paper with a skimmer, or your fingers, and put more in. If the syrup goes hard halfway through, cook it up again, adding a very little water.

Leave the candied violets to dry thoroughly before storing them. You may store them in glass jars, if you are going to use them all in a few weeks. Otherwise it is better to store them in a cardboard box, such as a chocolate box, putting them in layers separated by wax paper.

These make a charming surprise scattered over ice-cream, or on iced cakes, or served in tiny dishes after a dinner.

Violets you will find growing in the very gentlest of dips and hollows in woods and fields. If you find them growing near dusty roads, they will need to be washed first. There are various kinds of violets ranging in colour from white through lilac to the deepest of blues. And of course, there are yellow violets as well. The biggest violets I have ever found growing wild were up in the Georgian Bay district. Great clumps of them grew in the moist marshy hollows between the great rocks, well protected from such human predators as I by hosts of mosquitoes and black flies.

To take violets home from the country and keep them fresh, wrap them up entirely in wet newspaper.

You will not want many. The smallest of paper bags – the kind you get five cents' worth of candy in, would be ample for your wants, provided you are not going into the candied violet business. And if you are, we hope you will grow your own and leave the wild ones to small-time gatherers.

Sir Hugh Plat in his book *Delightes for Ladies* published in 1609, gives this interesting recipe. Note the vagueness of the amounts of ingredients, which leaves much (I think properly) to the ingenuity of the cook.

A WAY TO MAKE SUGAR-PLATE* BOTH OF COLOUR AND TASTE OF ANY FLOWER

Take Violets and heat them in a mortar with a little hard sugar, then put into it a sufficient quantitie of Rosewater, then lay your gum in steepe in the water, & so worke it into paste, & so wil your paste be both of the colour of the violet, and of the smell of the violet. In like sort may you work with Marigolds, Cowslips, Primroses, Buglosse or any other flower.

A few fresh violets sprinkled over a green spring salad add both charm and a subtle flavour.

Dandelions

Pick a peck of golden dandelion flowers the same day on which you wish to make wine from them. This should be an easy task, for what wild flower is more abundant? The time is May or June.

* A dainty kind of sweetmeat.

DANDELION WINE

1 gallon dandelion petals	*4 pounds sugar*
1 gallon boiling water	*1 tablespoon brewers' yeast*
1 orange	*or 1 cake compressed yeast*
1 lemon	*toast*

First pick the petals from the flowers. Or, to be more accurate, pick the little flowers from the flowerhead, throwing away the stems and the denuded heads. Put the flowers into a crock and pour over them the boiling water. Cover and leave for about ten days, stirring a few times during that period.

At the end of this time, strain, and put the liquid into a preserving kettle. Add the sugar. Peel the orange and lemon very carefully and thinly and drop the peel in. Then remove the white skin and the seeds and cut the fruit up. Put it into the kettle also. Boil the mixture for twenty minutes and return to the crock. When it has cooled, spread the yeast on the toast and put it in. Cover and leave for another two days. If you have a cask or a large five-gallon jar, pour the liquid into it, and bung up, or cork. (See Chokecherry Wine.) Leave it for at least two months, after which time you may bottle it.

Elderflowers

In June and July the elder puts forth its cloud of creamy white blossoms. Gather them when they are at absolutely full bloom.

ELDERFLOWER FRITTERS

Brandy; cinnamon stick; fat for deep frying; icing sugar; juice of half an orange; and fritter batter made so:

1 cup flour	2 eggs (preferably, but one
1 teaspoon baking powder	anyway)
¼ teaspoon salt	½-¾ cup milk

Sift together the dry ingredients. Separate the eggs. Add the beaten yolks and part of the milk, beating until smooth. The batter must not be too thick, so continue to add milk until it is creamy but not as runny as a pancake batter. Now beat the egg whites well and fold into the batter.

In the meantime, have the elderflowers prepared. Pour the brandy into a flat dish and put the cinnamon stick into it. Then lay the elderflowers, blossomside down, into the brandy and let them soak there for an hour. Swish them about occasionally if you are using only a small amount of brandy.

When you are ready to serve them, make your batter as above, dip the elderflowers into it, holding them by a short piece of stem which you will have left on. Drop them into the hot fat and let them turn golden. Remove to a hot platter, sprinkle them with the icing sugar and, just before serving, sprinkle the orange juice over them.

ELDERFLOWER WATER

Cover the blossoms with water (just) and bring to the boil. Boil for half an hour. Then strain. Let the liquid cool. Return it to the pan, measuring first, and add a cup of sugar for each pint of liquid. Boil ten minutes. Let it cool and then bottle.

You can use this as a flavouring agent or in making the following:

ELDERFLOWER ICE

2 cups elderflower	1 tablespoon lemon or
water	orange juice
1 cup sugar	grated skin of half an
	orange

Take two cups of elderflower water (or one, if this is all you have, and half the other quantities as well) and stir the sugar into the juice until it is all dissolved. Add the lemon or orange juice and the grated skin of half an orange. Put it into a refrigerator tray and freeze to a pleasant consistency.

The elderflower blossom is sometimes beaten into a cake batter to improve flavour, texture and, I believe, lightness.

Wild roses

Here are a few delicacies to make from wild rose petals.

CANDIED ROSE PETALS

You will have to do this very quickly after gathering the petals, otherwise they will begin to dry out.

1 cup sugar   *1 teaspoon rosewater*
¼ cup water   *rose petals*

Make a syrup of the sugar, water and the rosewater. Dip the rose petals slowly and carefully into the syrup, then lay them on absorbent paper and put them in a slightly warm oven to dry.

TO MAKE ROSEWATER

½ cup of water   *1 quart of rose petals*

Put half a cup of water in a pan with the rose petals. Bring it to a boil and let it simmer for at least fifteen minutes, covered, and another five uncovered. Strain, and funnel into a small bottle.

ROSE PETAL TEA

Gather the wild rose petals in the bud, put them into a box and let them dry in a sunny window, first unfolding the leaves from the bud so that they are fairly well separated. When they are thoroughly dried, keep them in a tin or jar.

When you make your tea, pour boiling water on a spoonful of the leaves, and serve if possible in tiny cups, clear, to get the full fragrance.

CHAPTER 3

Nuts

butternut

beech

hazel

Nuts

Autumn brings the lovely days of apple-ing, when you go from tree to tree trying, tasting, gathering the apples that are sweet and juicy for eating in one bag; the tart and juicy for cooking in another. It brings the time when you can strip the wild grapes from the vines and gather, at your peril, the rose hips for jelly or wine. And it can bring the pleasant task of gathering nuts.

The Beechnut

The beech is one of the few really beautiful trees undressed. The smooth grey trunk and coppery red of the stripped branches and twiglets against a late autumn-blue sky or a winter-whitened hill can make the heart sing.

It is said that a tree must be thirty years old before it bears nuts so when you go beechnutting in September, you look for the big, magnificently spreading trees. It is a very sensible idea to seek out the trees that grow on a hill, for in this way you will be able to reach the nuts on one side of the tree with little difficulty.

The beechnuts grow near the ends of the branches in the axils of leaves and are covered by a bur which splits open to reveal two small, shiny brown, pyramid-shaped nuts no longer than half an inch. With your thumb-nail you peel off the three sides of brown coating to get at the small, delicious kernel. A pocketful of beechnuts makes a fine nibble on a walk.

Anything you do with beechnuts besides eating them yourself, you do for love.

Hazelnut

The hazelnut grows on a bush or shrub about four to six feet tall along the edges of woods and roads. The outer covering of the nut is either like a fringed bonnet or a long beak which, when removed, leaves a brown-shelled nut a little over half an inch long.

The nuts are ready to pick in August.

CHICKEN BALLS IN HAZELNUTS

It is a good idea to have a lot more nuts than you would expect to use because, on those few occasions when I have found hazelnuts, I have cracked the shells only to find, in many cases, the wizened-up remains of a nut. However, you do not need a great many for this recipe.

1 cup cooked chicken pieces	*butter, flour, milk*
¼ to ½ cup hazelnuts	*salt, pepper, cinnamon, nutmeg*

Leave the skins on the hazelnuts and grate them in the blender. Then grind the chicken in the blender adding a spoonful of milk if necessary. For simplicity's sake I am presuming you have

a blender. Otherwise, of course, chop the nuts and grind the chicken as you normally would.

Melt a tablespoon of butter, stir in thoroughly a tablespoon of flour, and then add enough creamy milk to make a thick sauce – not a runny one. Add salt and pepper and a dash of cinnamon and nutmeg. Mix the chicken into the sauce and form it into ping-pong-sized balls.

Add about a quarter of a teaspoon of salt to the ground hazelnuts, then roll the balls in the nuts; they will stick on most satisfactorily. Set them in the refrigerator to cool and stiffen.

Melt a fair-sized piece of butter in a small frying pan and gently heat the balls, turning them around to get them nicely browned all over. I like them served simply on a mound of chopped, cooked spinach. It makes about a dozen balls which is ample for two and can be stretched to serve three.

HAZELNUT COOKIES

2 egg whites   1 cup ground hazelnuts
1 cup white sugar

Beat the egg whites stiff. Mix in the sugar and then the hazelnuts. Drop by spoonfuls onto a cookie tin and bake in a slow oven – about 225 degrees – for twenty to thirty minutes. If you really like hazelnuts, you will love these.

Black Walnuts

These days we seldom consider getting syrup from any tree but the sugar maple. In fact, you can tap the silver birch as well as the black walnut. But where you can find walnut trees in Canada nowadays on other than private property I don't know. If *you* do, then you can do all the things with them that you would normally do with walnuts.

"They prepared me some refreshment at this house, some excellent cakes, baked on the coals; eggs; a boiled black squirrel; tea and coffee made of peas, which was good. The sugar was made from black walnut trees, which looks darker than that from the maple, but I think it is sweeter."

Samuel Strickland: *Twenty-seven Years in the Canadian West*

Acorns

It was not until I learned that Indians used to eat acorns, usually by grinding them up and boiling them into a kind of mush, that I came to realize acorns were not poisonous. How that particular belief arose I do not know but it is still a popular superstition today.

Some acorns are bitter but others are edible and palatable. It is tannin that makes them bitter. To avoid bitterness it may be well to grind them and run cold water through them. The acorns from the White Oak, the Chestnut Oak, the Swamp White Oak and the Garry Oak in British Columbia, for example, may all be eaten.

A friend throws a handful of acorns, shelled, into her stew.

The following recipe I intended to try but when I went to gather the acorns I found they were wormy. I think it might work out well, however.

ACORN PATTIES

 1 cup ground acorns   ¼ cup sugar
 1 egg   salt, pepper
 ½ cup flour

Beat the egg, gradually add the sugar, then the seasonings, the
acorns and the flour. Then either bake them for ten or fifteen
minutes in a moderate oven or sauté them in butter.

The Butternut

The butternut tree grows along country roadsides or in woodsy
bits, often near water. You can pick it out from the other trees
by its long compound leaves composed of small, pointed, opposite leaflets.

By and by, the nuts appear in little clusters that look like
oblongish green miniature coconuts. One of the two times to
gather butternuts is when they are in this fuzzy green stage.

About the second week in July make for your butternut tree which, incidentally, you found and pinpointed previously in your memory or on a map or on the back of a matchbook that you kept around for ages but have now lost. Anyway, on the day you decide to go nutting, if you drive slowly along dirt roads or walk through likely-looking woods, you are bound to come upon some completely new butternut trees whose location you promptly pinpoint in your memory, or on a map, or on the back of a matchbook. . . .

A butternut tree is a tree, not a bush, and it stretches as tall as the maples and elms around it. You stand underneath and look up while your eyes become accustomed to what you are looking for – clusters of green nuts – and you become very excited as you see more and more. Like the rosiest apples and sundry other good things of this world, most of the nuts seem to be at the top of the tree or frustratingly out of reach. And who carries a ladder about with him? Butternut trees are seldom climbable which eliminates shaking down the nuts, so you have to devise other ways and means of getting at them.

The best I can advise is to find a long stout branch, preferably with a forked end, with which to flail about until you hit a clump. Eventually, you may just throw the thing in despair, but it does get the nuts down.

The reason you collect them at this stage is that you are going to pickle them. From now on they begin to turn woody as the hard shell forms beneath the husk. To make sure they are still soft enough for pickling purposes, run a knitting or a darning needle into one. If it goes in easily they are just right.

The whole thing, husk and all, is pickled to be eaten.

The outsides are a little sticky and furry and have a sweetly citric odour that you let stay on your fingers just for the pleasure of sniffing.

Gather as many as you can or want.

butternuts	*As many of these spices as*
1 quart malt vinegar	*possible:*
1 cup sugar	*2 teaspoons cinnamon*
salt	*2 teaspoons cloves*
	1 teaspoon mace
	1 teaspoon celery seed
	½ teaspoon black pepper
	2 teaspoons mustard seeds

Put the nuts in a crock and pour over them boiling hot water. Leave them half an hour, then wash them thoroughly under the tap. This should get the fuzz off.

Now make brine solution of one cup of salt to a gallon of water. Pour it over the nuts so they are covered and leave them in this for four days.

Mix the spices all together with a spoonful or two of vinegar and tie them in a fine muslin bag. Bring the vinegar to boil, add the sugar and the bag of spices and boil for 15 minutes.

Fill the sealers almost full of the rinsed butternuts. Pour the vinegar over them until the jars are filled to the top.

Leave them for a couple of months before using them. They and the liquid will have turned to a rich brown-black.

In the autumn keep an eye on your butternut tree (if you still have that matchbook) to see when the nuts begin to fall. With luck some of them will fall onto the road instead of into the ditch where they otherwise disappear forever amidst the tangle of goldenrod and asters and tall seeding grasses.

The main point about butternuts is getting at them. First you have the thick outside husk to remove, either by jumping on them or splitting them with a hammer. Inside you find a nut looking much like a walnut only smaller and more oblong and much harder to crack. Use the hammer.

BUTTERNUT SOUFFLÉ

1 cup (or thereabouts)   *½ cup sugar*
   butternuts   *½ cup cream*
¼ pound butter   *6 eggs, separated*

Chop the butternuts very finely (in the blender or otherwise). Cream the butter and add one at a time the yolks of the 6 eggs. Then add the sugar, the cream and finally the ground nuts, beating all the while.

Whip the egg whites stiff. Stir them into the other mixture. Pour the whole into a buttered souffle dish and bake at 375 degrees for an hour. Try to time it so that it will be ready exactly when needed.

BUTTERNUT SAUCE

If you have steamed some small trout to serve cold, you might like to dip them into this sauce.

1½ cups shelled butternuts   *½ cup olive oil*
small bunch of parsley   *salt, pepper*
some fresh tarragon if   *½ lemon, squeezed*
   possible or else dried

Put the butternuts, the de-stemmed parsley and the tarragon leaves in the blender. Add the olive oil. Season and add the lemon juice.

Traditionally, butternuts have been put into cakes as have hickory nuts. (Because I personally am unfamiliar with the hickory tree I shall not deal with it separately). In the following recipe from an old Canadian cookbook published in 1883, the nuts go into the filling instead.

66   *Hickory nuts*

"Ingredients – One and one half cupfuls of sugar, half a cupful of butter, a scant half-cupful of sweet milk, two cupfuls of flour, three eggs, two teaspoonfuls of cream-tartar, one of soda or three teaspoonfuls of baking powder.

Bake in layers. Filling for same: – One cupful of sweet cream or milk; let it come to a boil; then stir in one tablespoonful of corn starch which has previously been wet with cold milk, sweeten to taste; let it just boil up; remove from the fire, and stir in one pint of pulverized hickory [butternut] nut meats. Flavor to taste and when partially cool spread between each two layers."

Mrs. Clarke's Cookery Book (Toronto: The Grip Printing and Publishing Co. 1883.)

CHAPTER 4

Fish

```
                sunfish
                        smelts
            perch
                        whitefish
carp
                        catfish
```

Bass

"To dress Bass, and many other kinds of fish. Season
high with salt, pepper and cayenne, one slice salt
pork, one of bread, one egg, sweet marjoram, summer savory and parsley, minced fine and well mixed,
one gill wine, four ounces butter; stuff the fish –
bake in the oven one hour; thin slices of pork laid on
the fish as it goes into the oven; when done pour over
dissolved butter; serve up with stewed oysters, cranberries, boiled onions or potatoes."
James Macfarlane: *The Cook Not Mad* (1831)

This delightful recipe is found in what I believe to be the first
cookery book to be published in English, in Canada (Kings-
ton 1831). It will certainly reward the cook who follows it.

Bass, along with such fish as carp, pickerel, pike and perch,
need to be scaled. The easiest way to perform this operation
is to hold the head of the fish under the left hand and, with a
bluntish knife, work up against the scales from the tail towards
the head.

Carp

Only at the first of the season, when the water of the lakes is cool and fresh and the fish still lively, is it advisable to take carp.

Carp is, traditionally, stuffed. Descriptions of stuffed carp, together with the trimmings of the meal, by Gogol and other Russian writers, are equalled in detail and care only by Dickens' loving accounts of steak and kidney pie, or roast goose.

STUFFED CARP

Make a stuffing of:
> Breadcrumbs (2 cups approximately)
> seasonings, such as salt, pepper, capers, parsley, shallots
> cut up fine, an onion minced, thyme, a pinch of
> ginger, sage, tarragon
> 2 tablespoons butter
> ½ cup milk or tomato juice

Mix the herbs and spices with the butter, then add the other ingredients and stuff the cleaned, scaled fish with the mixture. Now, cut up several onions into round thin slices and lay them on the bottom of your baking pan. Place the fish on top of them. Rub the fish with butter and sprinkle it with salt and pepper. Lay over the top a piece of brown paper greased on both sides. Bake in a fairly hot oven 10-15 minutes per inch of thickness.

> *orange peel*   *onions*
> *ginger*   *cloves*
> *wine*   *boiling water*
> *stuffing as for stuffed carp omitting the breadcrumbs*

Use a large covered dish which may be put into the oven if you wish, or sat upon the stove. On a base of sliced onions sprinkle some orange peel and ginger. Lay the carp on this and add two cups of wine, or more if your fish is enormous. Stick an onion with cloves and put it in also. Add a cup or so of boiling water. Cover and cook slowly for two hours. If the sauce appears too thin, boil it up to reduce it. Strain it if you wish and pour it over the fish for serving.

Eels

> From a letter dated Montreal, June 14, 1684.
> "The inhabitants that are settled between Quebec and fifteen leagues higher, diverted me very agreeably with the fishing of eels. At low water they stretch out hurdles to the lowest water-mark; and that space of ground being then dry by the retreat of the water, is covered over and shut up by the hurdles. Between the hurdles they place at certain distances instruments called ruches, from the resemblance they bear to a bee-hive; besides baskets and little nets beflagged upon a pole . . . which are so overcrammed that they break."
> Lahontan's *Travels in Canada* from Pinkerton "Voyages and Travels," Vol. 13.

The problem with eels is overcoming the idea that they are snakes (they're not, they *are* fish) and then, skinning them. It is advisable to get a male friend or relative to do this for you. It will be a challenge to his hardihood and skill. If you are, already, a male friend or relative, of course you will do it anyway without question. In skinning, work from the tail towards the head.

EEL À LA SHEILA

1 eel weighing	*1 bottle of Burgundy or a*
2 pounds	*good red Canadian wine*
¼ pound large onions	*¼ pound small onions*
2 good tablespoons butter	*½ pound mushrooms*
1 heaping tablespoon flour	*seasoning*

Cut eel in pieces of an inch or so. Slice the large onions. Melt the butter and brown the onions. Add the flour to make a sauce, stirring, and slowly pour in the wine. Now put in the small whole onions, the mushrooms, sliced, and add the following spices: a little pepper, some cloves, nutmeg, ginger, cinnamon and salt. Cover and cook for three quarters of an hour. Then add the eel and cook for another hour and a half. Just before serving at the table, add a small glass of brandy, lit.

This is a truly delicious dish.

A method of cooking eels, dating back at least to the 16th century, is to 'spitchcock' them. Here is one recipe for

SPITCHCOCKED EEL

First skin and wash your eel. Then dry it on a cloth or absorbent paper, and sprinkle with the usual seasonings, plus some sage. Bring it around into a circle and skewer it. Now put it into your broiler, or lay it on a buttered grid in the oven, and

broil it until brown. Serve it with melted butter, fried parsley and balls of lemon butter.

FRIED EELS (an old Canadian recipe)

If small, they should be curled round and fried, being first dipped into egg and crumbs of bread.

EEL SOUP

Into a saucepan put: eels, water (one quart to each pound of eels); an onion, a bouquet of herbs; and boil them until the eels are soft and broken. Remove from heat and add 3 tablespoons of rich cream. Suggestion: toast some bread, cut into small squares and put a piece into each soup plate, pouring the soup over.

EELS IN TOMATO SAUCE WITH RICE

Stew your eels cut into pieces, in water or, better, in consommé, with lots of flavourings – I like bay leaves and tarragon.

Now you will need three cloves of garlic, a slice of butter about ½″ thick; a small tin of tomato paste, a glass of red wine, two or three sticks of celery cut up small, an onion, likewise cut up and some chopped parsley. Also, a half pound of mushrooms, peeled and sliced unless they are buttons, in which case just wipe them and leave whole.

Very gently stew the cut up slices of garlic in butter. This will make the most heavenly odour in your kitchen and you may want to stop right there – just tossing the eels in that and serving. However, presuming you want to go on; after the garlic has cooked about ten minutes, add the tomato paste, the wine, the celery and the onion, and let the sauce bubble around for

some time, covered. Peek at it occasionally, adding salt and pepper, parsley and a little more wine if it seems to warrant the addition. Taste to see if it is hot enough and sweet enough (add a spoonful of brown sugar if it needs it) and in general, make it to suit your taste. Incidentally, if you have no wine, use the liquor in which your eels have been stewing. Add the mushrooms and cook at least another ten minutes.

When the sauce is just right, and your guests are waiting, heap the rice (which you have foresightedly cooked in the meantime) on an enormous platter, arrange the eels atop, and pour the sauce over all. Your friends will be astonished, delighted and overwhelmed.

EEL PIE

2 eels	grated nutmeg
butter	1 tablespoon lemon juice
2 shallots	1 glass red wine or sherry
parsley, chopped	puff paste for the lid of
pepper and salt	the pie

Skin and clean your eels – probably two will be sufficient – and cut them into two-inch pieces. In a frying pan put some butter. Chop up the shallots, and let them stay in the butter, just barely heating, for five minutes. Add the parsley, pepper, salt, nutmeg, lemon juice and a glass of red wine or sherry. Put the eels in, and if they are not covered by the liquid, add enough water or wine to cover.

I hope you can make puff paste, because you must do so now, unless you have been very clever and purchased some at a bakery.

Now take a casserole or other baking dish, remove the eels from the liquid and lay them in the dish. If the sauce is not thick, and it probably won't be, thicken it a little by adding

butter mashed up with flour (one tablespoon of each) to the liquid and bringing it to a boil, stirring. Pour this sauce over the eels, and top it with a crust of puff paste. Bake it in the oven (375 degrees) for an hour or until the crust is done.

JELLIED EEL (or 'CHOLLIED' EEL as they say in London)

eels, unskinned
vinegar
gelatine

2 eggs, hard-boiled
seasoning

Boil the eel or eels in well-seasoned water and a dash of vinegar. When done, take out the eels and remove the skin and bones, and cut the eels into little pieces. Strain the liquid in which the eels were boiled, and boil it again, skimming every now and then to make it clear.

For each cup of liquid add a quarter-ounce of gelatine, boil together for a minute, then cool. Take a mould and arrange the pieces of eel in it, with some slices of hard-boiled eggs. Pour the jelly liquid very carefully, trying to preserve your arrangement, and put the dish into the refrigerator for four or five hours when it should be jelled and ready to turn out.

Catfish or mudcat

This is a fish spurned by many, enjoyed by some.

CURRY OF CATFISH

catfish
2 onions
1 tablespoon butter
1 heaping tablespoon flour

1 heaping tablespoon curry
  powder
1 teaspoon sugar
hot cooked rice

A catfish should be skinned. So first skin it, remove the head, clean and fillet it. Cut the fillets into thumb-sized pieces and cook them in a saucepan with plenty of water and a couple of sliced onions.

In a frying pan, melt the butter. Stir the flour mixed with the curry powder and sugar into the melted butter. Slowly add two cups of the water in which the fish has been cooked, stirring all the time. Bring it to a bubbling boil and let it thicken. Put the cooked fish into the sauce for a minute or two to heat, and then serve it with a dish of rice.

Maskinonge or muskilunge or muskie or lunge

> "The Lieutenant-Governor . . . announcing his intention of honoring me with a visit . . . assisted at my first dinner party in the Backwoods. There was a noble maskalongy. . . ."
>
> Thomas Need: *Six Years in the Bush* (1838)

This is a fish of many names, or at least of varied spelling, and I am sure I do not know which is official. However you spell it, your fish will always be a big one, since it mustn't be taken

under twenty-nine inches. You can bake it whole, using the recipe for lake trout, or you may like to do it the following way.

MUSKIE STEAK

butter	juice of half a lemon or
flour	1 teaspoon brandy
2 shallots	½ pound mushrooms or
2 cups chicken broth	1 tin of same
2 or 3 tablespoons tomato	1 egg yolk
sauce	3 or 4 tablespoons cream
salt, pepper, bay leaf, cloves	
and some minced parsley	

Cut your muskie into one-inch-thick steaks. In a large frying pan, make a roux of a walnut of butter and a heaping tablespoon of flour. Add two shallots cut up fine, stirring, and then stir in the chicken broth. When the sauce is smooth, add two or three tablespoons of tomato sauce, the seasonings and the lemon or brandy. Strain. Put the muskie steaks into the frying pan. Pour the sauce over and add the mushrooms. Cover with a lid for the first ten minutes and then cook for another five minutes with the lid off. At the last minute stir in the beaten yolk of an egg and three or four tablespoons of cream.

It will serve as many as you have steaks for.

Perch, sunfish and rock bass

The nice thing about a mess of perch or sunfish or rock bass is that you can nearly always catch them, which is more than you can say for lake trout, muskies and what-not. At least you can catch plenty of them when you don't want them.

FRIED PERCH

Scale the fish, remove the insides (or not, according to taste) and fry them golden. That is all you need to do for an on-the-spot mess of perch.

If you have flour, of course you can dip them in flour first, and seasonings.

This little fish *can* be filleted and the fillets fried, but it is a lot of work.

STEWED PERCH, for when you have a great many

perch	*nutmeg*
onions	*glass of wine*
ginger	

In a large frying pan or saucepan place the perch, having re-moved their scales, in careful layers. Between each layer put a layer of chopped onions sprinkled with ginger and nutmeg. Then add water half-way up, and a glass of wine, cover and cook gently until done – about half an hour.

FISH SOUP

small fish	*butter*
green onions	*1 tablespoon flour*
parsley	*1 cup cold milk*
savoury	*croutons and lemon*
salt and pepper	*for garnish*

This is a way of using various kinds of small fish, perch, sunfish and so on. Boil the fish until they begin to break up, and strain the liquid into another pot. Remove the skin and bones from the fish, and flake the meat. Return the flaked fish to the liquid to-gether with some chopped green onions, parsley, savoury and salt and pepper.

In a separate pan melt some butter, stir in a good tablespoon of flour and then a cup of cold milk. When the sauce is smooth, pour in the fish stock. Bring it to the boil, stirring. It is now ready to serve, with croutons and thin, thin slices of lemon floating on top.

Pike

Some fish should be eaten as close to their natural state as possible, in order to get their delicate flavour. Other fish – and pike in my opinion, is such a one – do not have much flavour, and are only interesting done up with a good sauce or made into a special dish. I know this statement is rank heresy to some and I hasten to add that pike *can* be a fine fish. The quality is very much dependent on the season and the water in which the fish is taken.

TO DISGUISE A PIKE – WAYS AND MEANS

FRITTERED

Cut the cleaned, skinned pike into pieces about three inches long and one inch wide. Season and dredge with flour. Then dip into a beaten egg and roll in breadcrumbs.

Heat some olive oil or butter if you are feeling reckless, or margarine or shortening if you aren't, and fry the pieces in it, not too many at a time.

These fritters should be served with a piquante sauce. I would suggest either a sauce tartare or a hot tomato sauce.

SAUCE TARTARE

Chop fine a few capers, parsley, one or two pickled gherkins, and some spring onions or chives. Add these to a cup or so of mayonnaise.

HOT TOMATO SAUCE (hot in the sense of seasoning)

Mix equal quantities of tinned tomato paste and mayonnaise. Add pepper to taste and serve in individual little dishes, so the fish can be dipped into the sauce between bites.

SWEETLY SOURLY

Cut the fish into small pieces about one by two inches. Use a large heavy skillet or frying pan with a lid. Cook the fish in a fair amount of salted water, with a lid on, for about 15 minutes. Cook it gently so that it will not fall apart. At the first sign of crumbling, remove the pan from the heat and the fish from the water. Keep the water, though. Now you require:

1 or 2 green peppers	*½ cup vinegar or pickle*
3 tablespoons cornstarch	*water, if pickles are used*
½ cup sugar	*or ½ cup pineapple juice,*
1 tin pineapple pieces or	*if pineapple used*
a small jar of mixed sweet	*1 tablespoon soysauce*
pickles	*½ cup tomato ketchup*

Cut up the green pepper into smallish pieces, and cook them gently in the fish-water while mixing the other things. Combine the cornstarch and sugar. Add soysauce, vinegar (or pineapple juice) ketchup and pickles (or pineapple). Add this to the fish stock in the frying pan and, stirring all the time, cook

until it comes to a boil and gets thick. Now, carefully deposit the pieces of fish in this sauce, and continue to cook gently, stirring, and making sure that all the pieces get entirely coated. Cook until the sauce is of the consistency desired: it can be fairly runny, or it can be cooked until it is adhering thickly to the individual pieces of fish. Naturally, one would suggest serving it with rice.

The next recipe comes from *Canadian Fish Recipes* put out by the Department of Fisheries, Ottawa (Consumer Bulletin No. 3). It is called:

BAKED FISH WITH PINEAPPLE, and seems to me a good way of preparing pike.

1 cup cubed, drained
pineapple
2 cups cooked, flaked
fish
6 tablespoons cream
½ teaspoon salt
⅛ teaspoon pepper

⅛ teaspoon paprika
1 cup mashed potatoes
1 egg, beaten
2 tablespoons milk
¼ cup grated, Canadian
cheddar cheese

Arrange cubed pineapple in a greased casserole. Add cream, salt and pepper to flaked fish and mix well together. Spread this fish mixture over the pineapple. Beat potatoes, beaten egg, milk and paprika until light and place over fish. Bake in moderately hot oven, 375 degrees, for fifteen minutes. Remove from oven and sprinkle top with grated cheddar cheese. Return to oven until cheese is melted, about five minutes. Yield: six servings.

Trout

> "Do not forget, however, when you have any of those trout weighing scarcely more than a quarter of a pound and caught in running brooks that murmur far from the capital – do not forget, I say, to fry them in the very finest olive oil you have. This simple dish, properly sprinkled and served up with slices of lemon is worthy of being offered to a cardinal."
>
> Brillat-Savarin: *Physiology of Taste*
> (2nd edition, 1838)

Here follow my favourite ways of preparing speckled, rainbow and brown trout.

FRIED

Trout are delicious dipped in breadcrumbs or flour and fried in butter, with plenty of salt and pepper sprinkled on them while they are frying. (A very simple, non-messy way of flouring small fish is to put half a cup of flour, with the seasonings, in a

paper bag. Drop the fish in, one or two at a time, shake vigorously, and remove.) Do not use a smoking pan, just medium heat, and put in only that number of fish which will not make for crowding. When the trout is browned on one side, turn and do likewise to the other.

The skin of the fish, when done this way, is deliciously crisp and tasty.

For a most pleasant accompaniment, split a banana in half (for each two people), fry it, and serve with the trout.

FRIED WITH BUTTER SAUCE

This will require the addition of more butter, some lemon juice, and some capers if you like.

Melt half a cup of butter and let it brown a very little. Add a teaspoon of lemon juice and the capers, and just bring to the boil. Pour this sauce over the trout which you have fried and arrange beautifully on a platter.

I have not said anything about *pre*-cooking preparation. The trout should be cleaned, but the head and tail may be left on to considerable effect. Some people eat the head, bones and all.

Incidentally, if you are serving up a large number of trout using the above recipe you will need more sauce. Just add an extra teaspoon of lemon juice for every extra half cup of butter, and a few more capers. Before serving, *try* the sauce; if it seems flavourless to you, add salt, or a drop of Worcester or tabasco or whatever you feel would improve it.

MY VERY FAVOURITE WAY — BOILED

I think there is no superior way to cook and eat small trout (say up to ten inches) than this:

Gather a fistful of clean whole mint. Lay it carefully and thickly over the entire bottom of a large, lidded frying pan.

Then place your little trout neatly on top of the mint and pour around them a half to one cup of water. Add some salt. Let them boil gently for five minutes.

Because of the small amount of water and the bed of mint, the trout are thus almost steamed.

These trout should be served cold, simply with a dish of mayonnaise. The mint flavour delicately penetrates into the flesh which is firm and delectable.

Do try it.

This is what a famous 19th century epicure and author, the Baron Brisse, says:

"They are so perfumed, these little trout, that it is sufficient to cook them in a light *court-bouillon* and as soon as they are perfectly cold to eat them *au naturel*; all seasoning detracting from their savour."

And

"*Truites au court-bouillon*. Clean the trout by the gills, dry them carefully, tie up the heads then cook them in a court-bouillon made of white wine seasoned with slivers of onion, sprigs of parsley, thyme, bay-leaf and salt, adding little bouillon; let them simmer until completely done, dry them, and serve on a napkin garnished with parsley. If a sauce is desired mix a part of the court-bouillon with butter and flour, reduce to half on a lively fire and serve."

Lake trout and large rainbow

BAKED

Parchment and silver foil are wonderful inventions and I use them gratefully when baking trout. Lay the cleaned whole fish

on the parchment or foil. Season it, dab it with several pieces of butter. Cut one or two tomatoes in halves or thick slices and lay along the fish. Then carefully fold the foil around the fish, making sure it is airtight. Put the package in a pan or straight into the oven as is.

For each inch of thickness through the body, cook your fish about twenty minutes.

This is a lovely way of cooking lake trout or large brown, rainbow, or speckled. The juices are kept in and should be poured over the fish when it is removed to a serving platter. It may further be garnished with lemon and is then ready to be served.

TRUITE AU BLEUE

At the time of year when you are fairly sure of catching several brook trout in the course of one fishing jaunt, and preferably if you can catch them close to home, you might like to try this delicate European dish.

So fresh should the trout be that I am informed when taken from the hook it should just be stunned on the head to unconsciousness and rushed to the pot.

Horrors, of course.

It is best there should be three of you for this performance: One to have the stock ready, one to catch the fish, one to rush from fisherman to cook.

Cook's Duty

In a good-sized pot bring to a boil two quarts of water, one cup of white wine or lacking that, ¾ cup of white vinegar with a teaspoon of sugar, an onion or two sliced, a bay leaf, a few peppercorns and a tablespoon of salt. Let it simmer.

Start this as the fisherman leaves the house, giving him a 20-minute start and the benefit of 10 minutes to catch his first trout.

To prevent nervousness while waiting, melt some butter, squeeze the juice of a lemon into it, add a few grinds of pepper and keep the resulting sauce warm.

On receiving the fish, dead or unconscious as the case may be, pop it into the simmering stock, put the lid on and turn off the heat. In about seven minutes, you can remove it to a warmed platter. Eat it as soon as possible.

Fisherman's Duty

Catch your fish as quickly as possible and never mind wandering up and down the stream for hours. Today you are fishing for the sake of eating fish, not for the sake of fishing.

Kill the trout or stun it, clean it as fast as possible and hand it to the rusher.

Rusher's Duty

Have a piece of foil ready to receive the trout so that you will not have to handle it unduly.

Run, don't walk, to the simmering pot.

Do not step into a groundhog's hole and keep your eyes peeled for roots or rocks which might send you flying.

If you fall, hang on to the fish.

You will be rewarded or punished according to your performance.

Pickerel

FILLET OF PICKEREL

Just in case you find yourself faced with filleting the fish all by yourself, here is how to do it:

Lay the fish on a flat board (if you are camping, the paddle of a canoe suits admirably). Use a sharp knife, such as a jack-knife; put it in at the tail, and saw your way up the backbone to the gill. Remove the fillet. Then turn the fish over and do the other side. The head, backbone, tail and entrails will all be in one piece. Now the fillets have to be skinned. Take one fillet, put it skin-down on the board. Start at the tail. Cut straight down to the skin, and then travel horizontally along (or rather, let your knife do so) to the other end of the fillet. Carefully remove the ribs which will still be adhering.

You now have almost boneless, beautiful fillets. Egg and flour or breadcrumb them and fry gently for a few minutes.

ROLLUPS (also for bass or other fish fillets)

6 fillets	½ cup breadcrumbs
juice of half a lemon	12 stoned olives
1 small tin clams	salt, pepper, basil

Sprinkle the fillets with lemon juice. Cut the clams up small (sometimes you can buy them already minced), and mix with the breadcrumbs, the cut-up olives, and seasoning. Put a spoonful or more at one end of each fillet and roll the fillet up, skewering it. The baking dish should be greased and well dotted with butter. Bake for about 20 minutes in a hot oven.

ROLLUPS IN TOMATOES

Make the rollups as above and pour over them a large can of tomatoes.

PICKEREL IN WHITE SAUCE

pickerel   *milk*
butter   *salt and pepper*
1 onion   *parsley or paprika*
1 heaping tablespoon flour

Fish must be boiled very carefully or else it will fall apart. Here silver foil is most useful.

You will need a fairly large saucepan in which you boil some water. Now prepare your fillets, seasoning them, adding a bit of butter on each fillet and one onion chopped very fine. Wrap them all together in the foil and put them into the boiling water for fifteen minutes per inch of thickness.

In a separate saucepan or frying pan, melt a walnut-sized piece of butter and stir in a heaping tablespoon of flour until it is smooth. Carefully undo the fish from the foil, pouring out any juices into a cup. Keep the fish warm on a platter in the oven. Now, add the juice to the flour, stirring all the time, and then gradually add milk, making up one cup of liquid altogether. Add salt and pepper and keep stirring until the sauce thickens and bubbles.

Pour it over the fillets, sprinkle with paprika, or chopped parsley and serve.

IN EGG SAUCE

Add one or two hard-boiled eggs, chopped up, to the white sauce, and serve as above.

Whitefish

"Whitefish . . . are most exquisitely good . . . they are so rich that sauce is seldom eaten with them, but it is a richness that never tires, it is so delicate a kind. They are usually boiled, or set before the fire in a pan with a few spoonfuls of water and an anchovy, which is a very good way of dressing them."
The Diary of Mrs. John Graves Simcoe (1792-1795)

FISH PIE

Fish pie is an unusual dish these days. You may like to try it for that very reason. You can use almost any kind of fish, muskie or bass being quite as suitable as whitefish.

fish, 2 or 3 pounds	*1 tablespoon vinegar*
1 pint rich milk	*parsley*
butter	*chopped yolk of an egg*
mushroom ketchup or	*pastry to cover*
* Worcester sauce*	

Boil the fish. You may boil it well, for you are going to remove the skin and bones anyway. When you have done so, you will need a wooden bowl or board and either a cup or a proper pestle. Pound the fish flesh up. Add a pint of cream or very rich milk, a lump of butter and a tablespoon of mushroom ketchup, or somewhat less of Worcester sauce. Add a tablespoon of vinegar, some chopped parsley and mix in well the yolk of an egg.

Put this into a pie dish and cover with pastry. Bake it for about half an hour.

Smelts

The exciting time of the smelt spawning run comes shortly after spring has arrived officially though not necessarily in fact. Smelts are caught chiefly in Newfoundland, the Maritimes and as far West as Ontario. Catching them is a nocturnal pastime and you use either seine nets or dip nets. With luck, you will come home with bushels of them. Here is an easy, pleasant way to prepare them:

FRIED SMELTS

Take four to six smelts per serving – or more, depending on the known appetites of those who are about to eat. Dip each fish in slightly beaten egg, *as is*, without cleaning it. Then run it through flour – whole wheat for preference. Lay the fish in a row in the frying pan and fry them until golden brown in butter or olive oil. Turn them only once.

It is not necessary to clean smelts, but if you insist, open them at the gills. Then draw each smelt between finger and thumb, beginning at the tail, to remove the insides.

CHAPTER 5

. . . . . and others

bullfrog

turtle

lamprey

Lampreys

It is said that Henry I of England, who had been quarrelling with his son-in-law while at Lyons, died of a surfeit of lampreys. Lampreys are still considered a delicacy in many European countries. In ancient times one Roman epicure cast a slave into his fish-pond to improve the flavour of his lampreys. And Julius Caesar once had three tons of lampreys served at a triumphal feast.

It is probably harder to catch a lamprey than it is for the lamprey to catch you – that is, if you happen to be a long distance swimmer with a predilection for crossing the deeper waters of the Great Lakes. The lamprey has done an incredible amount of harm to the Great Lakes fisheries and it seems only just retribution that we in turn have a go at the lamprey. It is for this reason that I add a recipe here for their cooking, because I must be truthful and say that I have never had occasion to eat one, nor to catch one.

The flesh is said to be white and tasty but highly indigestible (which may account for Henry I dying of a surfeit of them).

The recipes I've given for eels can be applied to lampreys. However, here is a slightly different one:

LAMPREY WITH VEGETABLES

lamprey	*3 carrots*
¼ pound bacon	*½ pound green beans*
⅓ pound fresh green	*1 small tin tomato juice*
* peas*	*salt and pepper*

Wash the lamprey well in warm water, and skin. Cut it into pieces about two inches in length. Now, take about a quarter of a pound of bacon and cut it up into small pieces. (Or you can buy bacon ends, at a much cheaper price, which are excellent for just such purposes as this.) Cook these together until the lamprey browns. Now add fresh green peas, carrots thinly cut or diced very small, and green beans cut into small pieces. Add a small tin of tomato juice with seasonings, simmer for ten or fifteen minutes until the vegetables are pleasantly cooked.

Francatelli was famous not only for writing some fine recipe books, such as *The Modern Cook*, but also because he himself became chief cook to Her Majesty Queen Victoria. Here, then, is his recipe which was, literally, fit for a queen.

LAMPREY EN MATELOTE

To wash lampreys it is necessary to put them into a large earthenware vessel with plenty of salt, with which they should be well scoured and afterwards thoroughly washed in several waters; by this means they are freed from the slimy mucus which adheres to this kind of fish. The lampreys should be trimmed and cut into pieces about two inches long, or they may be left whole, according to taste; they should be placed in a stew-pan with sliced carrot and onion, mace, peppercorns, thyme and bay leaf, parsley, mushrooms and salt; moisten them with a glass of port wine, and set the whole to stew gently on the fire. When done, take half the liquor in which the lampreys have been stewed and reduce it with half a pint of brown sauce;

add a glass of port wine, and as soon as the sauce is reduced to a proper consistency, incorporate with it a pat of butter, a little essence of anchovies, and lemon juice, and pass it through a tammy or fine sieve into a bain-marie containing some button-mushrooms, and stewed small button-onions. Drain the lampreys, place them on a dish, sauce them over with the ragout, and send to table.

Crawfish

It seems to me that I was told at school that crawfish are poisonous. I am not sure about this, and certainly do not wish to malign my biology teacher – so that the idea may just have come along with other old wives' tales.

At any rate, crawfish are edible. There is not a great deal of meat in them, but the novelty of serving an hors d'oeuvres of crawfish, or crawfish in sauce, makes up for quantity.

How do you catch them? I would suggest that the best way is to take a fly rod with worm bait to a small river and there pretend that you are fishing for rainbow trout. You are bound to catch one that way. This method is a trifle slow. In the small uncontaminated streams and rivers of this country the water is so clear that if you sit quietly on the bank, you can see down to the bottom where the crawfish lurk under large stones. If you move one of these stones quickly, you will probably be able to nab at least one of the big blue or green crustaceae.

They can be grasped by the back, about halfway between head and tail. To catch them easily, though, a small net or sieve is advisable. Dump them into a pail of water as you catch them. Another way of coaxing them into the open is to throw such things as fish guts into the water. You will probably see three or four slowly and cautiously converge on the food.

BOILED CRAWFISH

Have a quart of water with two tablespoons of salt in it, ready and boiling. Now quickly pop the live crawfish into the rapidly boiling water and cook for about twenty minutes. Remove them, and let cool. Serve them with slices of lemon, and mayonnaise in which to dip them.

You will have to remove the heads and peel the tails as with shrimps, before serving. The meat is in the tail.

CRAWFISH IN SAUCE

1 tin tomatoes
½ pound small mushrooms
butter or olive oil

bay leaf
1 or 2 onions chopped up
salt, pepper, paprika

Melt the butter and slowly fry the onion in it. Add the cleaned mushrooms, and the tomatoes. Cover and simmer for about half an hour. Then look at it. If it is very watery, go on simmering it with the lid off, while you get a pot of water boiling and cook your crawfish. Bring them together in a single dish and serve with either rice or a stick of French bread. The latter is handier for mopping up the sauce.

Mrs. Simcoe says that crushed crawfish is a cure for rattlesnake bite. I have never had occasion to doubt her word.

Turtles

> "Some small tortoises, cut up and dressed like oysters in scollop shells were very good at supper."
> *The Diary of Mrs. John Graves Simcoe* (1792-1795)

Mrs. Simcoe was not only one of the first gourmets ever to set foot in Canada but, I sometimes think, one of the most adventurous to this day. Of course, she did not have to prepare these tortoises (or terrapins as they may have been). But I rather imagine it would not have fazed her to do just that, *and* catch them too.

Turtles are sensitive to vibrations through their shells. Consequently it is not easy to capture them, even when you see dozens of them sitting on logs sunning themselves. I believe there are turtle traps. For the rest I leave it to your own ingenuity.

The turtle is killed by cutting off its head. The legs are skinned with a sharp knife, and the shell removed by cutting between the top and bottom shells. The turtle is then cleaned, i.e. the entrails are removed. The edible meat is provided chiefly by the flippers.

IN SHELLS

If you have tiny turtles and wish to serve them as Mrs. Simcoe was served hers at a banquet at Niagara in 1791, then of course save the top shells for this purpose.

Take the meat, dip it into egg, then breadcrumbs, and fry it in butter. When brown, lay the pieces in the top shells, keeping them warm in the oven. Sprinkle more breadcrumbs and melted butter over them, and serve with sliced lemon.

TURTLE STEW

turtle meat	*1 onion*
flour	*1 green pepper*
oil	*1 glass wine*
carrots	

If you have a larger turtle, a snapper for instance, cut the meat up into about inch squares. Roll it in seasoned flour, and brown it in oil. As it browns, drop it into a stew pan in which salted water is heating. When the turtle is all in the water, add sliced carrots, onion, rings of green pepper and a glass of wine. Simmer for a couple of hours.

Frogs' legs

There was a time when it was considered very peculiar indeed to eat frogs' legs. The French, who knew better, became known as a nation of frog-eaters and were given the opprobrious epithet, Frogs, by an unsympathetic and unimaginative world.

Bull-frogs and leopard frogs are the kind usually eaten. Here is one way to catch them. Using a rod and line, dangle an unbaited hook in front of the frog's nose. When you catch him you will be surprised at his extraordinary length, for he seemed such a lumpy squat thing sitting amongst the reeds waiting for flies.

It is the hind legs only which are eaten.

FROGS' LEGS IN GARLIC SAUCE

I think three pairs of frogs' legs make a good serving for one person. Skin the legs and soak them in cold salted water for a couple of hours. Dry them, dip them in flour and fry them slowly in butter for about fifteen minutes.

In another saucepan melt two tablespoons of butter per serving. Cut three cloves of garlic in halves and let it simmer away in the butter while the legs are cooking.

Serve the frogs' legs very hot, with the garlic butter ready to pour over them.

FROGS' LEGS IN BATTER

Season the legs, beat one or two eggs as required, dip the legs into the egg and then into cracker crumbs or oatmeal and fry in fairly deep fat.

FROGS' LEGS IN WINE SAUCE

frogs' legs	1 cup cream
(up to 8 or 10 pair)	salt and pepper
1 tablespoon flour	ground ginger
butter	glass of wine

Put the frogs' legs into boiling water for about three minutes. Remove, drain and dry, and then brown them quickly in a frying pan. Stir a tablespoon of flour into the melted butter, add a cupful of cream, salt, pepper and a dash of ginger, and a small glass of wine, stirring the while. Put the legs back in, and then remove the whole into a hot serving dish.

ANOTHER METHOD OF PREPARING FROGS' LEGS

boiling water	small bowl of lemon juice

Bullfrogs' legs may be rather tough. This method almost insures tenderness. Have a pan of water boiling. Hold each pair of legs for two seconds in the boiling water, dip them quickly in the lemon juice, then put them into the butter in a frying pan.

CHAPTER 6

Green vegetables

                              lamb's
bulrush   *quarters*
or cattail

                              milkweed

              mint

        watercress

                    plantain

Green vegetables and herbs

Most of us are really shockingly conservative people, one way or another, and our food and eating habits are not the least conservative and unadventurous things about us.

We prefer, seemingly, the known and therefore the safe things, with no thought of taking advantage (especially when in foreign countries) of exquisite new flavours and foods.

One country thinks another country barbarous because it does or doesn't eat porridge for breakfast; does or doesn't cool its toast before buttering; does or doesn't use rice as a vegetable; does or doesn't make coffee with hot milk.

In these matters children are most conservative of all (the sad thing, though, is that we so often hold on to our childish likes and dislikes throughout our lives). It may be extremely disappointing, therefore, to serve unusual foods to children. One way to make them interested in wild fruits and vegetables, though, is to take them with you hunting and gathering them.

If, however, they still refuse to eat watercress soup or Fiddle-heads au Gratin, then for goodness' sake don't waste them on the little horrors.

The difficulty about wild green vegetables is that usually they must be picked very young, when the leaves have barely uncurled and before any flower has appeared. This does make identification difficult, so unless you have a botanist in the family, or an excellent botanical guide, it is better to leave alone *anything of which you are unsure.*

However, there are some green plants which are unmistakable even in their infancy. One of these is the baby fern, or fiddlehead.

Ferns

You will find fiddleheads in cool damp woods. They may be six inches to a foot tall, with their fronds tucked in and their heads curled under like tight question marks. Cut or break them off in approximately even lengths of about four or five inches. Six to eight of these per person is an adequate serving.

about 3 dozen fiddleheads
1 cup shredded cheddar cheese
salt and pepper

Boil some water in a saucepan and put the ferns in it. Cook for ten minutes, and then test to see if they are tender. Another five minutes should certainly suffice. They must not be overcooked or they will be as horrid as asparagus is when *it* is overcooked. Add a good dose of salt.

In the meantime, shred some cheddar cheese, about one cupful. Drain the ferns, arrange them on a hot dish, put butter with them, pepper them and layer the cheese over the top. By the time they arrive at the table, the cheese will have melted the tiniest bit.

Depending on the type of fern, or bracken (pteridium aquilinum is edible) you pick, the vegetables will be more or less mucilaginous. This sounds horrible, but isn't particularly.

The fern is the magic plant which in former times was believed to bestow invisibility on those who knew how to use it properly!

BAKED FERNS

fiddleheads
salt
butter
3 tablespoons flour
1 cup stock or vegetable
  water

½ cup cream
1 egg yolk
2 tablespoons Parmesan
  cheese
½ cup breadcrumbs

Wash your fern heads. (Incidentally, they seem to be a very clean, insect-free vegetable.) Cook in boiling salted water for

ten minutes, until partly cooked. In the meantime, make a sauce by melting two or three tablespoons of butter; into which stir three tablespoons of flour, a pinch of salt, a cup of stock (or the water in which the ferns are cooking) and half a cup of cream. Then stir in the yolks of one or two eggs and finally two tablespoons of grated Parmesan cheese. Stir until all the cheese melts. Do this over a low heat.

Now, into a buttered oven-dish put the fiddleheads carefully in layers. Pour sauce over each layer; sprinkle a little Parmesan on each layer of sauce. Cover the top layer of ferns with sauce and sprinkle that with breadcrumbs. Put in a hot oven or under a grill for about twenty minutes, which should be long enough to brown the crumbs.

The Japanese, I understand, use fiddleheads in soup. That seems a most pleasant way of doing things. I think it should be a clear stock soup, or a consommé, with the tiniest of ferns floating around in it.

Those who like asparagus cold will probably like cold cooked fiddleheads also, with a French dressing or a lemon juice and oil dressing poured over them.

I myself prefer to toss yesterday's cold ferns about in a frying pan with plenty of butter, salt and pepper, until they are hot and browned.

Bulrush or cattail

It is the young flowerspike we seek, in the late spring before it has turned brown and sausagelike. To procure it, you may need to wear rubber boots or waders, for the bulrush grows in water-filled ditches and swamps.

At that time of year, the flower is still encased in its long

green leaf (it is rather like a very long, very thin cob of corn). To prepare it for cooking, peel it as you would corn. It will be of a dark velvety green colour and texture, and in two distinct divisions.

Put the flowers into boiling water for about ten minutes, when they should be cooked.

A little bowl of melted butter to dip them in, salt and pepper, and you have a treat.

The inside, by the way, is a hard core which you just nibble around.

The dandelion

> Dear common flower, that grow'st beside the way,
> Fringing the dusty road with harmless gold,
> First pledge of blithesome May,
>   James Russell Lowell

I think all gardeners and gourmets agree that there is nothing nicer and more satisfying than eating fruit and vegetables fresh from the garden. The gardener has it over the gourmet, though, in that he has pride of achievement, almost of creativity, as well.

One may perhaps have no garden but have a little lawn. There is something quite delightful in going to one's lawn to gather dandelions (and maybe fungi) for the coming meal. Not to have to buy *everything*, not to be completely dependent on others; perhaps that is part of the pleasure.

One usually thinks of the dandelion, if one thinks of it at all from a gastronomic viewpoint, as a salad green. But it can also be cooked as a green vegetable, like spinach. Since there is such an abundance of dandelions on lawns or in parks or

fields, it is only sensible to pick the smallest, cleanest, tenderest leaves. You may use the leaves even after the dandelion has flowered, changed from yellow to a grey-white fluff ball and finally blown away.

Always wash your dandelion greens first.

BOILED DANDELIONS

Toss a dishful of dandelion greens into a very little boiling salted water. Cook only long enough to make them tender but not into a pulpy mess. They will take lots of salt and pepper and butter when served. They go rather nicely with mashed potatoes and sausages; or on toast with poached eggs.

SAUTÉED DANDELIONS

Melt four tablespoons of olive oil or butter and add some chopped garlic. Then put in the dandelion greens immediately they have been washed, and cook ten to fifteen minutes. They will come out crisp and very tasty.

CREAMED DANDELIONS

a small bag of dandelions *1 piece preserved ginger*
1 tablespoon butter *fried croutons and*
1 tablespoon flour *sour cream for serving*
salt and pepper

Wash the leaves and cook well in boiling water. Then remove them from the water and chop them up small. Make a coating of sauce by melting a tablespoon of butter, mixing in a level tablespoon of flour and a tablespoon of stock (or water in which the dandelions have been cooked). Add salt and pepper, then stir in the chopped-up dandelion leaves. If you happen to have a tin

or jar of ginger in syrup, you might sliver up half a piece and put it in at this point.

Lay the dandelions on a plate of small fried croutons and put a dollop of sour cream on them.

SALAD

Dandelions, even the youngest leaves, are usually rather bitter. Consequently, the best way is to put a few dandelions into a tossed lettuce or mixed greens salad.

However, you might like to try dandelion salad proper. Use French dressing with garlic and a little sugar. Try tossing it with a handful of ripe olives. Or stir brown sugar into lemon juice and pour over the really chilled leaves.

IN SANDWICHES

Spread some thickly buttered slices of bread with a few drops of Worcester sauce, and then with chopped young leaves of dandelion.

DANDELION ROOT

The root when scraped well can be boiled in salted water for a fair length of time (at least half an hour, but of course until tender). It may be served seasoned, and buttered or with a white or cheese sauce.

A broth of dandelion roots, taken daily, was said to be good for the liver.

The flower, bless its shaggy yellow head, can be used in making wine, a recipe for which will be found under *Flowers*.

The early settlers knew and used the dandelion. Susannah Moodie, in *Roughing It In The Bush*, gives us yet another use.

In her day (around 1837) tea was not only exorbitantly expensive but an almost unobtainable luxury in many parts of Canada – a bitter trial, no doubt, to many English settlers. Mrs. Moodie tells us that she used both peppermint and sage in place of tea until, as she says "I found an excellent substitute for both in the roots of the dandelion, called 'dandelion-coffee'. Cut the roots into small pieces the size of kidney beans, roast them on an iron baking-pan in the stove until brown and crisp."

Mrs. Moodie used dandelion greens in salads – but she blanched them "to a beautiful cream colour with straw," and wrote that they made "an excellent salad." She said also that dandelion leaves can be "used early in the spring with boiled pork as a substitute for cabbage."

And how eagerly, after the long cold winter, with its monotonous diet of frozen fish and fritters and pork (if they were lucky) but no fresh green vegetables, must these early Canadian housewives have gathered the fresh greens from meadows and woods.

The dandelion even gave itself up to one further use, for in the township of Dummer (whether that township was unique in this respect I do not know, but doubt it) the settlers boiled the tops, added hops, fermented the whole and obtained a most excellent beer.

What more could one ask from one small plant?

Lamb's quarters

This plant generally grows in cultivated fields, and is usually considered merely a troublesome weed. In the spring and early summer, gather it when it is about six to ten inches high. If you like spinach, you are bound to like lamb's quarters.

BOILED LAMB'S QUARTERS

Like spinach, lamb's quarters should not be drowned in the process of being boiled. Wash the leaves very well, shake them and put them in the pot without further water. Cover the pot. Put them over a medium flame and let them cook about ten minutes. Drain thoroughly. Serve whole or chopped, with salt, pepper and a sprinkling of lemon juice.

WITH ALMONDS

To the cooked, chopped lamb's quarters add a quarter of a cup of almonds, which you have previously browned in butter.

LAMB'S QUARTERS FRITTERS

For a quite delightful change try this:

a bag of lamb's quarters   *2 eggs, separated*
  (about a quart)   *grated cheese*
nutmeg   *oil*
1 tablespoon butter

Boil the lamb's quarters, strain them well, then chop. Put into a bowl, grate a fair amount of nutmeg over them. Stir in a table-spoon of butter. Add the yolks of two eggs, stirring them in. Finally, mix in some grated Parmesan cheese. Leave the mixture to cool. When almost ready to serve, beat the egg whites and add them, and then drop the mixture by spoonfuls into hot deep fat or oil. Fry golden on both sides.

Milkweed

You will find milkweed growing in pasture fields and along the roadside. It is recognizable at a certain stage by the milk-

weed pods, which are ready for our cooking purposes about halfway through August. They will be a dusty shade of green, and should be no more than an inch to an inch and a half in length. You can easily gather enough to serve four people, as one plant will yield up to a half a dozen pods.

It is an exciting dish and I hope your guests will be duly appreciative.

BOILED MILKWEED PODS

Salt some water and bring it to a boil. Toss the washed milkweed pods in, and boil for ten minutes (but test, of course, to make sure they are tender). When you take them out, strain the water from them. Place them in a hot dish and sprinkle with salt, pepper and, if you like, some grated cheese.

I like to put a dab of butter on each pod as I eat it. I think you will find milkweed pods one of the most delicious green vegetables you have ever eaten.

Wild leeks

The wild leek is one of the very first things up in the woods in spring. You will find it in late April and early May, very likely before the snow has melted from the shaded places in the woods, and when the ground is still brown with last year's leaves and dead stalks.

It belongs to the lily family and you look for the typical broad leaf. It is a good idea to take a trowel or a spoon with you, as the bulb is below the earth's surface and you use the whole plant.

If you have once tasted wild leeks as a vegetable, you will scour the woods for them every April or May thereafter.

Parboil the washed leeks for five to eight minutes. Drain and finish by frying them, well salted, in butter.

Or, they are equally delicious merely fried in butter until they turn a dark brown. If possible, serve them atop a steak.

LEEKS AND CHEESE SAUCE

2 or 3 dozen leeks
piece of butter
1 tablespoon flour
1 cup milk

salt and pepper
nutmeg
4 ounces grated cheese

Boil the leeks about twenty minutes. Now make a cheese sauce thus: melt some butter, add a heaping tablespoon of flour, stir about, then add a cup of milk, stirring, then pepper and salt and some grated nutmeg. Finally, stir in the grated cheese.

Remove the leeks from the saucepan and place them in a buttered casserole. Pour over them the cheese sauce and put the dish into a hot oven, or under a grill, just long enough to brown the top.

Green vegetables   **115**

Wild mint

You will find mint growing close to the water along the gravelly banks of streams. Very likely you will smell it before you see it, sweet and refreshing as the cool spring streams it so often grows beside.

Mint has several other uses beyond mint sauce or mint juleps. For instance, a teaspoonful chopped up very fine indeed adds a piquancy to a summer salad. Or, two or three tablespoons of it, again chopped up and mashed into cream or cottage cheese, makes a good relish for hors d'oeuvres, biscuits or sandwich fillings, or a potato chip dip.

If you carefully dig up the root of a mint plant and keep it moist until you get home, you will be able to plant it in a pot or in your garden so that you can have fresh mint whenever you want it. It first appears in the spring and continues on during the summer.

Mint sauce, of course, is traditional with roast lamb.

MINT SAUCE

Wash the mint well and mince it fine. Use enough to make three tablespoons when chopped. Add two tablespoons of sugar and three quarters of a cup of vinegar. Let this sit for at least half a day before using.

This is enough only for one dinner. Very likely you will want to make enough to bottle some for the winter. A good idea is to use a vinegar bottle or empty wine bottle.

Chop up a great deal of mint (even the above recipe may not be thick enough for your taste, in which case, of course, the remedy is plain. There are those who feel that mint sauce

should be all mint, with only enough vinegar to moisten it and make it pourable). Put two or three tablespoons of fine sugar over this, and pour over the whole some vinegar. (White wine vinegar is usually recommended although I rather like the darker types myself.) Then funnel it into your bottle, adding enough vinegar to fill it, cork and keep in a cool place.

It is a very happy coincidence that lamb and tiny new potatoes appear at the same time – and just when the mint is coming up.

The very tiny marble-sized new potatoes are not sought after for some reason unfathomable to me. I can only think that people feel it would be too much trouble to scrape them. But in fact, it would be a sin to do so. The skin is delicious and potatoes can be rubbed clean, in water, with one's thumbs or a scrubbing brush.

In the boiling water, together with your potatoes, put at least two entire sprigs of mint. The flavour permeates the tiny potatoes which are absolutely delicious after being drained, sprinkled with salt and pepper and tossed about in butter. I would certainly advise cooking lots and lots of them because they are as good cold as they are hot, especially when served with mayonnaise.

Mint added to new green peas makes for an excellent flavour. And as mentioned elsewhere, it should be used in plenty when boiling small trout.

MINT JELLY

This is a very nice way of preserving mint for winter use. You can make the jelly clear, without the mint in it, or you can leave some of it in.

1 cup mint leaves	1¼ cups water
pressed down	1½ pounds sugar
½ cup vinegar	

Wash the mint. Mince it very well, and place in a saucepan. Add half a cup of vinegar and one and a quarter cups of water. Bring it to a boil. Remove from the heat and let stand for a few minutes. Now you may strain it, leaving in some of the mint if you like (it looks rather pretty in the jars). Put one and a half pounds of sugar into this liquid, mix well and bring to a boil. Continue to boil it for twenty minutes, then test on a plate to see if it will set. Boil longer if it needs it.

This makes a delicate-coloured jelly. If you want it to be green, to prove that it is mint jelly, you will need to add a little green colouring-matter after you have put in the sugar and while you are bringing it to the boil.

GRAPE AND MINT JELLY

4 pounds grapes	sugar
1 bunch of mint, minced	

Crush the grapes and the mint, cook them until pulpy, then strain. Put through a sieve to get rid of the stalks, skins and pips and then put the resultant liquid through a jelly-bag.

Now, however many cups of juice you have, match them with an equal number of cups of sugar. Heat the juice, boil five minutes, then add the sugar and boil for another five minutes. Then bottle.

MINT RELISH

½ cup mint leaves	¾ lb. raisins
1 lb. apples	6 small onions
1 lb. sugar	1½ quarts vinegar
½ cup salt	1 ounce white mustard seed
10 tomatoes	

Chop everything up together, including the flavourings. Boil the vinegar, after which let it cool. Add it to the mixture and put it all in a crock, letting it stay there for a week to ten days, stirring it daily. It is then ready to be put into bottles and sealed.

MINT VINEGAR

For this you will need a plentiful supply of mint, some vinegar, a wine or vinegar bottle, and a jar or wide-mouthed bottle. Crush the mint and *fill* the jar with it, then pour in your vinegar until the bottle will hold no more. Let it stand for five weeks, at which time you can strain it into the wine bottle. Try it in an oil-and-vinegar dressing on tossed salad greens.

You can also make a very useful and delicious mint chutney.

MINT WINE

3 pounds sugar
1¼ gallons of water
yeast

2 quarts mint leaves packed down (try to remove as many of the stems as possible)

Make a syrup with the sugar and water, bringing it to the boil. Crush the mint leaves into a crock and pour over the hot syrup. Cool to 65 or 70 degrees and add your yeast; then cover with Saran Wrap and keep down with an elastic or string.

Leave this to ferment for two or three weeks, watching it ferment and noting when the fermentation stops. At that time, strain it into either gallon jars or back into the cleaned crock. Leave it for a week or so and then bottle.

Cool, it makes a delightful wine on a hot day.

MINT CHUTNEY

1 cup mint
1 cup raisins
½ teaspoon salt

cayenne
3 tablespoons vinegar

Wash a large bunch of mint and pick the leaves off. Measure them, then chop them fine. To the quantity of chopped mint (about a cup) add an equal quantity of raisins, and chop them too. Put in a half-teaspoon of salt, a little cayenne, three table-spoons of vinegar and mix. Using a tumbler or a cup, pound the mixture to a smooth paste. When you feel it is as smooth as you would like, put it in little jars and cap.

A SLIGHTLY DIFFERENT RECIPE

mint	*2 tablespoons sugar*
1 onion	*salt, black pepper and*
2 cooking apples	*cayenne*

Chop and pound the mint (a goodly sized bunch of it) together with the onion. Add the apples, chopped up, and finally the sugar, salt, pepper and cayenne. It is ready for use or bottling.

MINT AND RHUBARB CONSERVE

1 quart rhubarb, when	*4 cups chopped mint*
cut up	*4 cups sugar*

Wash and dry the rhubarb and cut it into small pieces. Put them into a saucepan with the sugar and mint. Cook until thick, and bottle. This is interesting served with meats.

CANDIED MINT

The trick in candying mint leaves is to make sure the mint is absolutely dry when the syrup is poured on. After washing the leaves, it would be very well not only to pat them dry, but to leave them exposed to the sun for a few hours.

Make a syrup of two cups of sugar to half a cup of water, cooking it until a soft ball forms when dropped in a glass of cold

water. Grease a pie plate or large flat dish. Stir the syrup and then pour over the leaves. Let them stand a while, turning once or twice to make sure they are completely crystallized.

MINT ICE

1 quart boiling water
2 cups sugar
½ cup finely minced
  mint

grated rind and juice of
  1 lemon
½ cup of a tart jelly or the
  juice of another lemon

Boil the water and sugar together for five minutes. Pour over the mint and let cool, then strain. Add the remaining ingredients. Chill, then transfer to the freezer until firm.

Plantain

The plantain is a ubiquitous weed growing on lawns and in vacant lots. As a child you may have plucked the single leaf and, pulling it like a Christmas cracker with a friend, discovered from it how many lies you had told in the past, or how much gold you might expect in the future.

Like most wild green things, these leaves should be plucked very young and tender, in the spring.

SWEET AND SOUR PLANTAIN

a bagful of plantain
  leaves
3 strips of breakfast
  bacon

¼ cup of vinegar
1 tablespoon sugar
1 egg, hard-boiled (optional)
salt and pepper

Cook the plantain in two waters and drain when cooked (about fifteen minutes). Chop the bacon into small squares and fry it

until it is crisp. To the bacon add the vinegar, water and sugar. Add seasoning and heat it to the boiling point. Arrange the plantain in a hot dish and pour the sauce over it. Garnish with the egg, sliced very thinly.

Marsh marigolds

One of the first wild flowers to be up and doing in the spring is the marsh marigold. I remember a walk in my early teens with my cousin to the woods, shivering in the cold raw air of spring, with a sun which tried to smile but was unable to put much fire behind it. My cousin astride a rail fence, suddenly calling "Look, look! Gold!" My sweet cousin loved to be dramatic, but truly it *was* a carpet of gold, a veritable El Dorado gleaming up from the dark green leaves and darker, danker marsh water. And how delicious then, to gather great luxuriant bunches, knowing that here nature was prodigal and would mint thousands more of the golden coins.

When the leaves are small you may gather them, with their stems, for a green vegetable. Also pick the tiny green clusters

of flower buds. You can use them, too.

Word of warning: do not eat the leaves raw. They must be cooked to be edible.

When you get home, wash the leaves and stems thoroughly. Then, in a very small amount of boiling salted water, boil the marsh marigolds until they appear to be cooked. I prefer them, like spinach, still to have their shape, which means that their texture will be on the firm side rather than the soggy side. Salt, pepper, butter them and serve.

Or place them, cooked, in an oven-proof dish, sprinkle generously with grated cheese, preferably Canadian Cheddar, or Swiss cheese, which you yourself have grated. Pop under the grill, or in a hot oven for five minutes.

CREAMED MARSH MARIGOLDS

butter   *salt and pepper*
1 tablespoon flour   *paprika*
1 cup milk

Cook the leaves and stalks for a few minutes. Prepare a cream sauce by putting a walnut of butter in a saucepan, melting it, adding a tablespoon of flour and stirring well. Then, before it has time to burn, add up to one cup of milk slowly, stirring all the time. Salt and pepper. Add the cooked and drained marsh marigold leaves and stems. Mix well, pile into a hot dish, and sprinkle with paprika.

PICKLED FLOWER BUDS

You may or may not have cooked the flower buds with your greens. It is perfectly all right if you did; they are quite delicious. But you might like to pickle them as capers in the following manner:

Green vegetables **123**

Having washed the greenery, remove the buds. Put them in a bowl with some salted water for a couple of hours. In the meantime, put some pickling spice into a small muslin bag, and put *it* into some vinegar which you will bring to a boil. Have some very small glass jars ready. Drain the capers, and fill the jars with them to about half an inch from the top. Then fill the jars to the top with the boiling spiced vinegar. Cap.

Capers may be used as and with hors d'oeuvres. Or you can now make a caper sauce to go very nicely with fillet of sole or leg of lamb.

CAPER SAUCE 1

Melt a quarter-pound of butter. Add one small jar of your capers (or as many as you think fit) together with a good dollop of the vinegar juice. Simmer and serve.

CAPER SAUCE 2

1 tablespoon butter	salt and pepper
1½ tablespoons flour	1 cup milk
2 cups stock or	capers
consommé	

Melt the butter in a saucepan. Stir in one and a half tablespoons of flour. Add the stock or consommé, salt and pepper, and milk. Stir until the sauce thickens and bubbles. Remove from the fire. Stir in as many capers as you like, with a spoonful of the juice, and serve in a sauceboat.

SAUCE TARTARE

If you are making a quick Sauce Tartare to serve with fish, add chopped capers as well as chopped pickles to a cupful of mayonnaise.

Chicory

Chicory (often erroneously called cornflower) makes beautiful our summer meadows and roadsides with the deep vivid blue of its flowers.

It is in the spring, before the flowers have appeared to help us identify it, however, that we use the plant. The leaves are long and deeply indented or toothed. These you may boil, changing the water during the process to get rid of any bitterness. Before serving, season well and stir in two tablespoons of heavy cream.

SALAD

The young tender leaves may be used in salad, and are usually blanched for this purpose. This is possible only if you live near a field of chicory. If you are fortunate enough to do so, you can blanch the leaves by covering the plant with a flower-pot for two or three days.

Watercress

You will find watercress from late spring through summer, in slow-moving streams, ditches and pools. Try to get it from moving water rather than from stagnant ponds or ditches, and wash it very well, using several waters.

Watercress gives a cool, yet peppery flavour to salad.

It may also be used, cooked, as a green vegetable. Indeed, the ancients ate watercress boiled in goat's milk and believed it to be a cure for insanity.

BOILED WATERCRESS

Put the well-washed cress into half a cup of boiling salted water for ten minutes. Drain it, chop it up and return it to the saucepan with a walnut of butter, seasoning, and a teaspoon of lemon juice. Very pleasant served with croutons.

CREAMED WATERCRESS

Make a sauce by melting a tablespoon of butter and mixing in it two of flour. Add a cup of stock and stir to a boil. Season, adding a little lemon juice. Now, put in the watercress which has been thoroughly washed and chopped. Boil this for a few minutes, stirring, and it will be ready to serve.

ANOTHER WAY

Wash in two or three waters a goodly bunch of watercress. Shake it only a little and put it into a saucepan without any more water. Sprinkle with salt. Heat slowly for twenty-five minutes. Drain, keeping the water. Chop fine. Roll in flour a

piece of butter the size of a walnut, and put it in the water which you have kept in the saucepan. Bring it to the boil, add the cress and slowly stir until thickened.

SALAD

watercress French dressing
hard-boiled egg dry mustard

Lay your watercress in ice water until crisp. Then dry thoroughly in a wire basket or napkin. Put the watercress in the salad bowl. Chop the hard-boiled egg fine, and sprinkle it over the salad. Serve it with a French dressing which has a little dry mustard added to it.

GREEN SALAD WITH WATERCRESS

Use watercress in equal quantities with lettuce or endive. Tear the lettuce leaves and the watercress into your salad bowl. Cut up a green spring onion into tiny pieces and add it. Then toss the salad with a French dressing.

Indeed, watercress may be added to most tossed salads with profit. However, watercress and tomatoes together also make a pleasant salad, with either an oil-and-vinegar dressing, or with mayonnaise.

And of course, watercress laid on thin slices of brown or white buttered bread, with salt, pepper and mayonnaise, makes scrumptious sandwiches. Watercress is excellent in sandwiches in combination with cream cheese or peanut butter.

WATERCRESS SAUCE

Remove the stalks from a bunch of watercress (washed, of course). Put the leaves into a saucepan with a pint of milk, a

pinch of salt. Let it boil up two or three times until the cress is tender, then drain and press out the moisture. Chop it up, mix in a tablespoon of butter, and pass it through a sieve.

Now melt a tablespoon of butter with one of flour, and add gradually three quarters of a pint of the milk in which the watercress was boiled. Bring this to a boil; strain it and mix it with the sieved watercress. Keep it warm for serving.

This is a good sauce for fish.

WATERCRESS SOUP

Boil two potatoes in about one and a half cups of water. Season with salt and pepper and add chopped watercress leaves and top stalks. Boil, covered, for half an hour, then put it through a sieve. Add a little milk when serving and, to make it especially nice, add a spoonful of butter to each bowl of soup.

Wild grape vine leaves

Long before the wild grapes are ripe for picking, the leaf can be used. Look for the cleanest, largest, choicest leaves, if you are interested in cooking an exotic dish of stuffed vine leaves.

STUFFED VINE LEAVES

1 cup cooked rice
½ pound very finely
ground meat: veal, beef
or lamb

seasonings such as basil,
tarragon, salt and pepper
2 or 3 dozen vine leaves

Mix together the ingredients, with the exception of the vine leaves. Have some water boiling. Now dip the leaves into the

water, even leaving them there for a few seconds – long enough to take the crimp out of their style. Then put a spoonful of the mixture into the leaf and fold it over, tucking in the edges. Place it, fold side down (to keep it in place), in a casserole or shallow oven dish. Fill the bottom of your dish, packing the rolls in tightly. If you have more, lay them very carefully on top of the others. Now you can add a little water. Or, to make the dish tastier, mix the juice of two lemons with some brown sugar, about half a cup, and pour this over and around the rolls. Another pleasant sauce is made by pouring over the rolls a tin of tomato soup with the juice of a lemon added to it. Finally, cover the dish and bake for about an hour.

Sorrel

"It is one of ye wholesomest herbs that can be eaten, being antiscorbutic, resists putrefaction, creates appetites, represses bile and allays thirst."

There are two completely different plants bearing this name. One, the Sheep or Field Sorrel (Rumex), is considered an annoying weed and is therefore to be found in cultivated fields. Its basal leaves resemble those of the dandelion.

The other, Wood Sorrel (Oxalis), is a wild flower found chiefly in sheltered woods. Its leaves resemble those of the shamrock.

They both make an excellent soup. In Europe, sorrel is dressed as spinach, and very often added to spinach to provide a complementary flavour.

SORREL SOUP

Take two large handfuls of sorrel and wash it well. Remove the stalks. Melt a piece of butter in a frying pan and add the sorrel leaves. Stir them until they become a greenish-brown.

Now boil in a saucepan two peeled potatoes. When they are cooked, put them through a sieve. To this purée add the sorrel, with salt and pepper. Put back in the saucepan and add about three cups of milk and a spoonful of butter. Heat it and serve.

Wood sorrel is fun just to nibble on, and because of its lemony flavour it is a pleasant addition to salads.

Mrs. Simcoe says: "The Indians near the coast . . . prepare the (salmon) roes beating them up with sorrel, a plant with acid taste, till it becomes a kind of caviare and, when the salmon are dried, boil and mix them with oil."

This information was brought back to her from what is now British Columbia by the famous explorer, Alexander Mackenzie.

CHAPTER 7

Root vegetables

wild salsify

Root vegetables

There are many edible roots of wild plants. Most of them, though, should be treated as emergency foods only, either because they tend to be bitter anyway, or because they support a flower which is attractive and not too plentiful. Therefore we would not use, except perhaps to satisfy our curiosity, the trillium, the day lily, the jack-in-the-pulpit.

The following plants are easily identifiable, but again I would say, *never* eat the greens, root, or berry of a plant, and cerainly never eat a fungus, of which you are not absolutely sure.

Wild salsify

This plant is also called oyster-plant because of a reputed similarity in flavour between it and oysters, a similarity which I have not particularly noticed. Salsify grows along the roadsides, sometimes in fields, to a height of two or three feet. The flower is yellow, resembling a dandelion, and the leaves are long and narrow. Try to collect the root before the flower blooms, for otherwise the pith will be tough and uneatable. It is a pleasant, sweetish vegetable, somewhat similar to the cultivated parsnip.

BOILED

Scrape the roots clean and boil them in salted water for fifteen minutes or longer if necessary.

MASHED WILD SALSIFY

Boil as above, and then put the vegetable through a coarse sieve. Add salt, pepper, a spoonful or two of milk or cream and a dash of lemon juice.

LEFTOVER BOILED SALSIFY

Cut the cold cooked salsify into strips or rounds, and fry in butter.

Wild ginger

Wild ginger grows in clumps in rich woodland soil. It is identified by the pair of heart-shaped leaves borne on its sturdy, hairy stem and, of course, by its aromatic root. Early summer is the time to look for it and it is advisable to carry along a trowel with which to dig it up.

Wash the wild ginger and soak it in cold water overnight. Make a thick syrup using two cups of sugar to a scant cup of water. When it is clear, put in the wild ginger and boil until it is fairly tender. Remove the wild ginger and boil the syrup down further unless it is already good and thick.

Keep the wild ginger in the syrup, in a bowl, or, if you have enough, bottle it.

This may be eaten as is. Or, for a delicious dessert, slice bananas over ice-cream; cut up a piece of candied wild ginger into tiny bits and sprinkle over the bananas. Pour a spoonful of the syrup around each portion.

Arrowhead

This plant is to be found in shallow ponds and marshes. You will need to wear high rubber boots to pull up the root. The leaf projects an arrow-shaped blade above the surface of the water, and the flower is white. Late summer is the time to try for the root.

BOILED ARROWHEAD

Collect the roots. Put them into boiling salted water and let them cook for half an hour or more. When they are tender, remove them and, holding them with a fork, remove their skins.

In a saucepan, melt some butter. Chop some fresh parsley fine, add it to the butter, and then toss about the arrowhead roots (or tubers, to be perfectly correct) until they are coated with butter and parsley. If any is left over, pour it over the arrowheads in the serving-dish.

CHAPTER 8

Game

squirrel

        deer

            beaver

muskrat

Game animals

If you are thinking of trying any of the unusual game animals, such as raccoon or squirrel, beaver or muskrat, be sure to find out the game laws, which vary not only from province to province and year to year, but also from district to district. At the moment, for instance, there may be an open season on both raccoon and porcupine in your region, and you may need only an ordinary dollar licence to shoot these animals. On the other hand, if you wish to try that delicacy, beaver tail, you will need a trapper's licence, as both beaver and muskrat may be trapped only, and that in season.

I feel that there is often a wicked waste of meat of the fur-bearing animals, when they are taken for their fur. Of course if the carcasses are left for other animals they are not wasted. Nevertheless, it would be an interesting change to have raccoon, muskrat and beaver in the shops occasionally. The objection which applies to game and wild fowl being sold in shops would not apply here, since these animals are already taken for their fur.

Beaver

"the Lieutenant-Governor announcing his intention of honoring me with a visit . . . assisted at my first dinner party in the Backwoods. There was a noble maskalongy, suppported by the choice parts of a couple of bucks; then for *entremets*, we had beaver tails (a rare delicacy), partridges, wild fowl and squirrels. My garden supplied the dessert-melons, plums, strawberries and apples."

Thomas Need: *Six Years in the Bush* (1838)

That was, surely, an elegant bachelor dinner for the backwoods of 1834, yet one taken almost entirely from the forest and streams. Beaver tails were considered a delicacy formerly, though I have not met anyone who thinks highly of them now. However, at a recent (January 1962) banquet of the Beaver Club, which is a modern counterpart of the early 18-century Montreal Association of Trappers and Voyageurs, beaver tails were made into presumably excellent soup, well flavoured with herbs.

I find that beaver meat is a cross between goose and veal – dark and fat like the former, but tender and dry like the latter. It is very pleasant eating, but I have had it only in a kind of stew or fricassee. Here is how I did it:

beaver meat	2 carrots
flour	1 stick celery
oil	1 green pepper
2 chopped onions	6 miniature tomatoes

Chop the meat into small pieces, removing the fat. Dredge with flour. Brown the pieces very quickly in hot oil, and as they cook remove them to a saucepan containing boiling salted water. Now, add chopped onions, sliced carrots, celery if you wish, a green pepper cut up, and later on, half a dozen tiny tomatoes. Simmer this for an hour and a half or thereabouts. Serve as stew.

If you can, when you are given (or have caught) a fresh beaver, soak it overnight in salt water. At the Beaver Club banquet, the body meat was minced and marinated and then made into delicious cup-cake sized tourtières.

BEAVER PAW FOR ENERGY

"Take the paw of a freshly killed beaver in one hand and pat it with the other, saying – 'Please, may I be like you'. This insures that the man or woman will always work hard, like a beaver."
T. F. MacIlwraith: *Bella Coola Indians* (1948)

Porcupine

"It is a most delicious dish not unlike sucking pig, but with much more flavour."
John Langton: *Early Days in Upper Canada*

Because of the damage the porcupine does to the trees, it is not protected and may be taken at any time. It is another meat which is extravagantly wasted, since most people shoot porcupines as nuisances but leave their flesh.

The best way to cook porcupine if you are out in the open is the old method used by early hunters and Indians. That is,

to roll it as it is, quills, intestines and all, in a thick coating of clay and mud. It can then be put right into the centre of an open fire and baked for a lengthy period (two hours at least). When it is removed from the fire and the hard clay is taken off, the quills and skin should come off too, and the porky be ready for eating.

However, there are other, more convenient ways of cooking porcupine. They do, alas, involve skinning and gutting the animal but fortunately, contrary to what one might think, you do not have to pluck the quills one by one; they come off with the skin.

ROAST PORCUPINE

Make some stuffing by mixing a tablespoon of herbs into a tablespoon of butter, and putting that into soft breadcrumbs.

Stuff the porcupine, salt and pepper the skin and roast it, covered, for one and a half to two hours.

The best and most meat is on the hind legs. If you have several of the animals, you can use the following recipe:

BARBECUED PORCUPINE HAUNCHES

2 good sized haunches
1 medium onion, chopped
½ cup celery, chopped
1½ teaspoons prepared
    mustard
2 tablespoons brown sugar

2 tablespoons vinegar
juice of 1 lemon
small bottle of ketchup or
    tin of tomato paste
water
salt, pepper

Parboil the legs for half an hour in salted water, while making the sauce.

Brown the onion in butter, add the celery. Mix together the mustard, sugar, vinegar, lemon juice and a cup and a half of water, the entire bottle of ketchup, and the seasonings. Then put them in the pan with the onion and celery and simmer gently for one hour.

Put the legs into an oven dish, pour the sauce over them and cook in 350 degree oven for another hour at least. If the sauce does not cover the legs, baste and turn them occasionally.

Muskrat

Peter Kalm, the famous Dutch biologist and traveller who visited Canada just before the Seven Years' War, wrote: "Nobody here eats their (muskrat) flesh. I do not know whether the Indians eat it, for they are commonly not over nice in the choice of meat. The musk-bag is put between the cloaths in order to preserve them against worms."

However, muskrat is considered very fine meat. It is small enough to be fried. You can use the same recipes for cooking muskrat as those which follow for rabbit.

Groundhog

Groundhogs are supposedly best for eating in September and October, but we had one caught in May and enjoyed it. This is how I did it.

Cut the groundhog (which someone else has skinned and gutted for you – this is IMPORTANT) into serving pieces and soak it in salted water for at least an hour. Then rinse it in fresh water and make a marinade:

1½ cups red wine	*1 or 2 onions sliced*
a few peppercorns	*½ cup vinegar*
1 or 2 carrots	*3 tablespoons oil*
1 cut-up garlic clove	*1 bay leaf*

Put the groundhog pieces in this and marinate in the refrigerator for twenty-four to forty-eight hours.

At the end of this time, remove the pieces onto paper towelling to dry. Fry them in butter or oil until browned all over. Strain the marinade and add to the frying pan. Cover and cook very slowly for an hour and a half or even two hours. Thicken the juice if you like with a little flour.

In a separate frying pan, brown some big, whole mushrooms and some small brown onions.

Put the meat on a platter, surround with the mushrooms and onions and pour the sauce over all.

Rabbit and hare

Flopsy, Mopsy, Cottontail and Peter Rabbit were told, if you remember, *not* to go into Mr. MacGregor's garden lest the same fate befall them as befell their father – namely, they might end up in a rabbit pie.

Rabbit pie is only one thing which might happen to a rabbit. It might, for instance become –

ROAST RABBIT

1 rabbit	1 egg
1 cup breadcrumbs	1 tablespoon sugar
2 sticks celery, chopped	1 teaspoon ginger
cinnamon	¼ teaspoon each cinnamon
4 slices bacon	and mace

After having skinned and cleaned the rabbit, and removed all the shot, wash it well in cold water and rinse it in lukewarm water. Now let it sit for one to three hours covered, in cold water to which a teaspoon of salt has been added.

Remove and wipe it well with a clean cloth. Stuff it with a dressing of breadcrumbs, a little chopped celery, cinnamon, and an egg to bind it. Truss it up. In a cup, mix the ginger, a little cinnamon and a little mace. Then sprinkle this over the outside of the rabbit. Over this lay the slices of bacon.

Roast it for an hour and a half or longer, to make it pleasantly brown, and serve with gravy. Wild grape or cranberry jelly will be delicious with it.

RABBIT DINNER

rabbit	3 carrots
4 slices bacon	3 or 4 potatoes
2 onions	salt and pepper

This is an unstuffed way of roasting rabbit. Prepare it for roasting as above. Having dried it, arrange it in a roasting pan which contains some oil. Also put bacon along the back.

Into the pan put peeled onions, carrots, and potatoes cut into quarters if they are large. Sprinkle the rabbit and vegetables with salt and pepper, and put into a hot oven.

Watch the oven and if things seem to be drying out, add a cup of hot water. Cook for an hour to an hour and a half (350 degree oven).

There are those who hold up their hands in horror at the idea of frying game of any kind. I think rabbit, however, fries well, in the manner of chicken. There are two ways of going about this. One is to fry it direct, as it were, and the other is to boil it for a few minutes first, if you think it is rather elderly.

If you decide to boil it first, pop the whole rabbit into boiling water for ten minutes, then remove it, cut it into serving pieces and let it cool. If you do not boil it, break the rabbit up into serving pieces and marinate them in salted water for four hours.

FRIED RABBIT

rabbit cut up	salt and pepper
breadcrumbs	¼ cup butter
1 beaten egg	¼ teaspoon sage
milk	¼ teaspoon parsley

Dry the pieces of marinated or parboiled rabbit. Have ready breadcrumbs or cracker crumbs, and a beaten egg with a small

amount of milk added to it. Salt and pepper, of course. Melt a quarter cup of butter in a frying pan, and add a quarter teaspoon of sage and a quarter teaspoon of parsley. Dip the pieces of rabbit into the egg and then into the breadcrumbs, and put them into the very hot butter, cooking until brown and then turning. Then lower the flame, cover, and continue to cook for fifteen minutes to half an hour, adding a little more butter if necessary.

RABBIT IN WINE

1 rabbit
Marinade:
1 cup red wine
1 cup water
2 onions sliced thin
2 bay leaves
2 tablespoons olive oil
2 stalks celery
1 carrot sliced thin
thyme
salt and pepper

butter
1 tablespoon butter
2 tablespoons flour
½ pound sliced mushrooms

When you clean your rabbit, keep all the blood. Now, cut the rabbit into serving pieces and put the pieces into the marinade. Do this the day before you intend to serve it, or even the day before that.

About one hour before the actual time of serving, remove the rabbit on to absorbent paper. Melt some butter and brown the pieces in it, turning them occasionally. Add some sliced onions or else a couple of dozen tiny whole onions, and let them brown. Strain the marinade. Sprinkle the flour around the rabbit and onions in the pan, then add as much of the strained liquid as possible, and water or wine if the pieces are not covered. Add the sliced mushrooms, cover tightly and cook for an hour.

Check during this time to see that there is plenty of liquid.

Add the blood, and make sure the rabbit is cooked by testing with a knife. If the knife enters the flesh easily the rabbit is cooked. Serve in a hot deep casserole.

RABBIT PIE

a rabbit	*2 or 3 potatoes, diced*
1 onion, minced fine	*a fine rich crust*
some minced parsley	*flour*
some bacon ends	*2 hard boiled eggs, sliced*

Cut the rabbit into two or three pieces and boil in salted water to cover, along with the onion and parsley. Cook it gently until tender, and then remove the rabbit from the pot. Take the meat from the bones.

In a large skillet melt a walnut of butter, add about 2 tablespoons of flour, stirring well, and then pour in the liquid in which the rabbit was cooked, until you have a nice thick gravy. Now, if you have plenty of crust pastry, line the bottom and sides of a dish with it (you will need more for the top). Lay in a few pieces of rabbit, then some potatoes, the rest of the rabbit and the rest of the potatoes. Also, the slices of hard-boiled egg. Pour the gravy over this, and top it all with a lid of crust. Bake it for an hour in a medium oven.

Did you get lots of rabbits or hares this year? Then perhaps you would like to try this old recipe.

HARE'S EARS

Take as many pairs of ears as your dish will contain; scald them well, and braise them till tender; add a glass of wine, and a slice

or two of lemon; when done, take them out, dip them in a thick batter and fry them. Serve with any relishing sauce.

Squirrel

"The flesh of the black squirrel is excellent eating, far superior to that of the rabbit."
Samuel Strickland: *Twenty Seven Years in the Bush* (1853)

Both the black squirrel *and* the grey are good eating. If they are small and young, cut them into pieces suitable for frying, and proceed as in the recipe for *Fried Rabbit*. If older, then they are better made into

SQUIRREL STEW

2 or 3 squirrels	6 carrots
flour	1 green pepper
oil	1 tin lima beans
1 tin tomatoes	salt, pepper, tarragon,
3 or 4 onions	chopped parsley

Cut the squirrels into small pieces. Toss them in flour, and brown them in two tablespoons of oil. Remove them to your stew pot. Pour over them the tin of tomatoes. Cut up three or four good-sized onions and add them. Add thin rings of carrots and green pepper, and plenty of flavourings. Cover and simmer any length of time over two hours. Half an hour before serving, add the tin of lima beans.

Venison

> "The venison in Canada is good and abundant, but very lean, very unlike English venison; the price is generally 4 or 6 cents a pound."
>
> Anna Jameson: *Winter Studies and Summer Rambles* (1838)

Let us suppose you are fortunate enough to have the deer cut up for you by the butcher. Then you will be handed in neat packages the various cuts: the roasts, the steaks, the stewing meat and the ground meat.

On the whole, one can proceed as for beef, with two differences: some cuts of venison should be marinated; and the gravy or sauce is all-important.

> ". . . we had a grand banquet on venison-steaks fried with ham, and potatoes in abundance; and a better dish I think I never tasted. Venison pie and soup, for days after, furnished quite a treat in the house."
>
> John C. Geikie: *Adventures in Canada* (1879)

VENISON STEAK

Melt butter in a pan, and broil steaks of about an inch thickness, quickly on both sides. Salt and pepper them well and serve with balls of lemon butter.

VENISON STEW

You will probably wish to use your own favourite stew recipe. Here's mine, for venison:

   Put 3 tablespoons oil or fat into a stew pan and heat. Put a good half-cup of flour into a dish, and mix in salt, pepper, pinch of ground cloves and a pinch of cinnamon. Cut the venison into small pieces, roll it in the flour and brown it in the oil. When all the pieces are nicely browned, pour over them a tin of tomatoes. Cut two or three carrots lengthwise into quarters or sixths and add them, together with rings of green pepper, then at least a quarter of a pound of mushrooms, sliced if they are large, or whole if they are buttons. Add half a cup of red wine. Simmer for an hour. If the stew is too wet for your liking, cook with the cover off for another twenty minutes or so. Before serving, you might float very, very thin slices of lemon on top.
   The ground venison may be made into patties or meat loaf.

VENISON PATTIES

Season your meat, form into patties, and brown on both sides in oil. Then pour around them a brown gravy and let them simmer gently in it for half an hour.
   Or, instead of gravy, try a can of tomato soup, with the juice of half a lemon added.

VENISON LOAF

1 pound ground venison
seasonings
½ cup carrots, grated
½ cup oatmeal or
   breadcrumbs

1 egg
1 dozen stuffed olives
3 strips bacon, or
   1 can mushroom soup

To a pound of seasoned meat, add the grated carrots, the oat-meal or fine breadcrumbs, an egg and a dozen stuffed olives. Lay strips of bacon over the top of the loaf, or pour over it a can of mushroom soup with a small amount of water added, and bake in a 375 degree oven for an hour.

WITH MACARONI

1 cup macaroni
4 slices bacon
minced venison
1 green pepper

mushrooms – up to 1 cup
1 cup tomato juice
1 small tin corn Niblets

Cook a cup of macaroni while preparing the meat. Fry three or four slices of bacon crisply, letting them break up. Then brown the venison thoroughly in the bacon fat, breaking it up and turning it well with a fork. A green pepper cut into squares could now be added, and mushrooms if you have some. Pour over these a cup of tomato juice and, to make a complete meal, add a small tin of corn Niblets. When ready to serve, pour the meat mixture over the hot macaroni.

VENISON LIVER

Fry some bacon. When it is cooked, remove it from the pan. Cut the liver in thin slices, dredge with seasoned flour and fry in the bacon fat.

ROAST VENISON

Like beef, venison should be well hung and served rare. The lesser cuts, such as the leg, should be marinated for several hours at least, in a bottle of red wine, salt, a few peppercorns, a clove or two of garlic, and a bay leaf. (Or a large bottle of gin-

ger ale is a simple and effective marinade.) Turn the meat a few times in the marinade. Remove it from the liquid and cover it thoroughly with strips of bacon or fat. Baste it during the roasting and allow about twenty-five minutes per pound in a 350 degree oven.

GRAVY FOR ROAST VENISON

Make your usual brown gravy, but add a few cloves and some ground nutmeg.

Or, if you want to make the occasion of a roast of venison a truly memorable one, you could serve a really interesting gravy, and I know of no better one than –

FRANCATELLI'S SAUCE FOR VENISON

Bruise one stick of cinnamon and twelve cloves, and put them into a small stew pan with two ounces of sugar and the peel of one lemon pared off very thin and perfectly free from any portion of white pulp; moisten with three glasses of port wine and set the whole to simmer gently on the fire for a quarter of an hour; then strain it through a sieve into a small stewpan containing a pot of red currant jelly. Just before sending the sauce to table, set it on the fire to boil, in order to melt the currant jelly so that it may mix with the essence of spice, etc.

CHAPTER 9

Fungi

puffball

chanterelle

Mushrooms and other fungi

A friend of mine went with me gathering a variety of fungi. Upon our arrival home, we cooked ourselves a delectable dish of them. My friend's sister would have no part of the feast and expected to see us keel over with each mouthful. This is an unfortunate attitude which would preclude many original and delicious dishes from your menu.

The other foolish attitude towards fungi is the opposite extreme: carelessness. It is far, far better to leave a mushroom sitting in a field if you are unsure of it, than to take a chance; because one poisonous mushroom would be quite sufficient to polish you off.

Since there are many more edible and harmless species than noxious ones, it would be well to learn thoroughly the appearance of the latter. There is no rule of thumb to go by – a gold ring does *not* necessarily turn black when rubbed on a poisonous mushroom; nor does colour mean anything; the red Emetic Russula is poisonous but the Scarlet Hygrophorus is edible; the white field mushroom is delicious and edible but the white Deadly Agaric is as deadly as its name implies.

However, to avoid all mushrooms because some are poisonous in nonsensical. One should invest in a good guide book

on the subject, with pictures and full descriptions. Two excellent books are *Edible and Poisonous Mushrooms of Canada* by Walton Groves, put out by the Queen's Printer, Ottawa, in 1961, and *Mushrooms of Eastern Canada and the United States*, by René Pomerleau, Chantecler Press. Apart from books such as these, there are Government pamphlets from time to time.

The ancient Romans were fond of mushrooms but were unscientific about them. Hence they were constantly being disposed of by mushroom poisoning.

In actual fact, they may have had more science than I am giving them credit for, since more than one Caesar was brought to an untimely end by a dish of poisonous fungi – prepared, it is said, by their wives. Nero's mother, for example, secured the throne for him by poisoning off his father with just such a dish.

Two edible species which are easily identifiable are the puffball and the morel. When collecting them, avoid picking old ones. Puffballs, when old, will be easily pokeable instead of hard, and a really old one will send out a smoke of brown spores when your finger penetrates it. Other edible fungi *look* old when they're old – that is, hole-y, collapsed, spotted, wrinkled and, when broken, wormy.

The puffball

The puffball, which may be as small as a golf ball or as large as a pumpkin, is usually to be found sitting like a round white stone in a grassy meadow or field. Just remove it carefully from its base and take it home as quickly as you can before anyone else claims it.

When you get your puffball home, scrape off any soil cling-
ing to it and wipe it thoroughly with a damp cloth if it is small.
If it is a large one, peel it.

THE EASIEST WAY, YET PLEASANT, OF PREPARING PUFFBALL

Melt some butter in a frying pan. Cut the puffball with a sharp
knife into fairly thin slices and put them into the butter, which
should not be very hot. Now sprinkle generously with salt and
pepper. When brown on one side, turn, and salt and pepper the
other side. This makes a fine luncheon dish served with bacon.
   A large puffball goes a very long way.

BATTERED PUFFBALL SLICES (by which I mean in bat-
ter, not bruised and beaten)

Cut the puffball into very thin slices, then into strips, and run
them through a slightly beaten and well seasoned egg. Put them
into breadcrumbs and finally fry them.

CREAMED PUFFBALL

2 cups of puffball, diced   *½ cup heavy cream*
butter   *salt and pepper*
flour   *nutmeg*

Dice the puffball and sauté it in a generous portion of butter,
but slowly. Dust it with flour, and stir well. Then add the half
cup of thick cream, salt, pepper and a grating of nutmeg. Cover,
and keep for a few minutes at low heat. This may be served as a
side dish (sprinkle with paprika before serving) or on toast as a
snack.

To make a dish for lunch from this recipe, add some chopped cooked ham and a small glassful of sherry. Let it all bubble gently for a few minutes, then fill hot patty shells and serve.

ONIONS WITH PUFFBALLS

Fry one pound of thickly sliced onions in butter, slowly. Add two cups of sliced puffballs. Cook together gently for five minutes.

PUFFBALL IN VERMOUTH

puffball sliced   *clove of garlic*
vermouth

Fry the sliced puffball in butter. Then cover the slices with vermouth, add a clove of garlic cut in two, and simmer gently for ten or fifteen minutes.

PUFFBALL WITH SOUR CREAM

puffball   *sour cream*
2 or 3 chives

Slice the puffball thin and fry. Now stack the slices in an even pile, putting between each layer a sprinkling of chopped chives and a layer of sour cream. Press together, and stack until you have a pile about five inches high. Then, using a sharp knife, cut into half- or three-quarter-inch slices, and serve.

The lovely thing about mushrooms is that they need never go to waste, for no matter what you are cooking, you can add mushrooms to it. Stews, meat loaves, soups, gravies are all enriched by the addition of mushrooms.

Different species have different habitats, and it is best to

refer to your guide book for information. However, it is wise to keep your eyes open wherever you are. Also, various species appear from spring until well into autumn.

The morel which appears in May is usually found in semi-woodland areas; the field mushroom with its fat rounded white cap is found in pasture fields and has also been known to grow *on the road*, amongst the stones and pebbles at the side. If you find a certain kind once, you will go on finding it in the same place year after year.

The fungi that grow on your front lawn, which spring up magically overnight, are edible too, though somewhat soft in consistency. They are the Coprinus family, and may be Inky Caps, Shaggy Manes, or Glistening Coprinus. They usually grow in very thick clumps and look like lots of toes seen from underneath. People sometimes foolishly kick them all down, fearing that their cat or dog or their child will eat them and be poisoned.

From here in I will let the word mushroom cover all the edible fungi without giving separate recipes for the different species. Some of them, such as the field mushroom, will need to be peeled before cooking, whereas the chanterelle, Inky Cap, and morel, for example, will only need to be washed or wiped. Morels, which look like long tiny sponges with hollow stems, are best fried in butter with perhaps the juice of half a lemon squeezed over them just before serving. Also, *I* soak them first in cold water, well-salted. I daresay it is squeamish, but I do like to be sure that all the inhabitants or visitors caught in the indentations when the morel was picked will leave it before I eat it.

The softer fungi of the Coprinus family are delicious stewed gently in a few tablespoons of butter, in a covered saucepan, for about twenty-five minutes.

Now here are a few of the numerous ways the mushroom (which is a highly nutritious food, by the way) may be prepared.

MUSHROOM SOUP

1 onion
3 tablespoons fat
½ pound mushrooms
  (about 2 cups)

3 pints water
1 potato, cubed
1 tablespoon meat extract
¼ cup sour cream

Peel and slice the mushrooms.

Chop the onion and fry it in three tablespoons of fat. Add the mushrooms. Add three tablespoons of water, and simmer gently, covered, an hour and a half, stirring occasionally and adding a little water if necessary. Then add three pints of water and the cubed potato. Boil for 20 minutes. Add meat extract. Remove from the heat and drop in the sour cream just before serving.

A SHORTER AND JUST AS NICE RECIPE FOR SOUP

½ lb. mushrooms
soup stock or a tin of
  bouillon
1 pint milk

seasoning
1 tablespoon butter
1 tablespoon flour
½ pint whipped cream

Cut up the washed mushrooms and boil them in the soup stock for half an hour. Take out about half of them and chop them up very fine, or mince them. Add the milk to the soup stock, season to taste and thicken with the butter and flour rubbed together. Now put in the finely chopped mushrooms, and serve the soup topped with whipped cream.

For a quickly prepared soup, partly out of a can: Add paper-thin slices of mushrooms and the green tops of celery, chopped, to a tin of consommé or beef bouillon. Just as it comes to the boil turn the heat low, drop in a raw egg and stir it vigorously for about a minute. Serve with fried croutons. This is a delicious Chinese-y soup which is improved by the use of various of your favourite herbs as well.

Mushrooms, whole if small or sliced if big, are always a most welcome addition to a stew if you happen to be making one.

MUSHROOMS AS VEGETABLES

If you are in a hurry for a vegetable (in other words, want to use a tin of something) but at the same time you wish to serve a slightly different dish, this is very pleasant:

1 tin corn Niblets   *mushrooms – as many as*
                               you have gathered

Lightly fry the mushrooms, cut in halves (or quarters if they are very large), letting them remain plump. Make sure you don't leave them unattended for long, or you will return to find them all shrivelled up. Then, heat your Niblets in a saucepan, add the mushrooms, toss together and serve, with a sprinkling of paprika. If the Niblets are plain, half a green pepper sliced into thin strips and fried with the mushrooms completes a delicious dish.

MUSHROOMS AU GRATIN

butter   *¼ cup sherry*
1 to 2 cups mushrooms   *1 cup cream*
salt and pepper   *nutmeg*
flour   *grated Parmesan cheese*
1 cup milk

Prepare your mushrooms. Melt some butter and add the mushrooms. Sprinkle with salt and pepper, and brown gently for ten minutes, tossing occasionally. Remove the mushrooms. Add a good tablespoon of flour to the butter, stir, then slowly pour in a cup of milk, a quarter cup of sherry, and a cup of cream. Sprinkle with grated nutmeg. Stir very briskly until the sauce just comes to the boil. Add the mushrooms, lower the heat, and cook slowly for ten minutes. Transfer to a casserole and sprinkle with grated Parmesan. Dot with butter, put in the oven ten minutes and the dish will be ready to serve.

MUSHROOMS WITH ONIONS AND SOUR CREAM

a small bagful mushrooms   *¼ cup of milk*
1 onion, chopped   *½ pint of sour cream*
1 tablespoon butter   *salt and pepper*
2 tablespoons of flour

In one frying pan, sauté the chopped onion in a generous amount of butter.

In another, melt a tablespoon of butter, stir the flour into it well and add the milk, stirring until smooth. Pour the onions into this and add the mushrooms. Sprinkle with salt and pepper. Slowly add half the sour cream, stirring it in. Let the mushrooms cook gently for about five minutes. Then add the rest of the sour cream until it is hot.

STUFFED MUSHROOMS

If you have found some good-sized mushrooms, this is an excellent way to use them.

Remove the stalks, but of course don't throw them away. And if you peel your mushrooms, wipe them well with a damp cloth first and save the peelings. Later, when you have time, stew the peelings in butter, in a covered pan. Then bottle them. In winter you can use them for sauces or stews.

You will be using the stalks later in this recipe. If you have washed your mushrooms, wipe them dry. Now heat them, for a couple of minutes only, in a tablespoon of butter. Remove to a plate and sprinkle with salt and lemon juice.

Now, chop the stalks very fine. Chop up one or two shallots, a slice of raw ham (chopped fine or ground) and brown them all in butter, easily, stirring frequently. Then add a tablespoon of flour, stir, and pour in a cupful of cream or rich milk, salt,

and pepper a-plenty. When the mixture comes to a boil, add two tablespoons of breadcrumbs and one egg yolk, and mix and heat the whole for three minutes. Remove. Cool. Stuff the mushrooms and place them on an oven-proof platter, gill sides up. Put them in a hot oven for five to eight minutes.

STUFFED MUSHROOMS 2

large mushrooms	*butter*
1 onion, finely chopped	*1 cup stock*
few sprigs of parsley	*½ cup breadcrumbs*
other herbs	*2 tablespoons grated cheese*

Chop the peeled mushroom stalks small, and add to them a finely chopped onion. Add some minced parsley and any other herbs you particularly favour, and fry the mixture in butter. Then add a cup of stock (or tinned beef bouillon or consommé if you have no stock on hand) and some breadcrumbs. When this thickens to the right consistency fill the hollow depression of the mushrooms. Sprinkle with breadcrumbs or grated cheese. Bake in a quick oven.

STUFFED MUSHROOMS 3

I have served each guest a single mushroom, stuffed, with its stalk still upright like an opened, upturned umbrella, as a tiny separate course. For this, a slice or two of bacon was fried, with chopped onion and breadcrumbs. Everything should be chopped or crumbled very fine. The bottoms of the mushrooms were browned. Then the stuffing was carefully packed in the hollow around the stem and they were popped into the oven for the duration of the previous course. A single large mushroom per person is quite enough. It can also be used as a savoury at the end of a meal.

166   *Morels*

STUFFED MORELS

After all, it *is* necessary to add a special recipe for a special fungus. You will notice that the morel is cunningly contrived to have both a hollow head and a hollow stem – perfect, in short, for stuffing. For this purpose you will have to wash the morels well (rather than soak them) and dry them thoroughly. Then, make a forcemeat stuffing of sage, minced veal and breadcrumbs. Stuff the morels with this, right down through the stems, brush with melted butter, sprinkle with salt and pepper, and bake for half an hour.

BAKED MUSHROOMS

Butter well some slices of bread and sprinkle with salt and pepper and anything else you think would be nice. Place on the

bread some clean mushrooms, stem side up, with bits of butter on their gills. (Remove the stems if you think it looks nicer.) Bake about 30 minutes in a medium oven.

CURRIED MUSHROOMS

I would suggest this only for the less tasty mushrooms, such as Inky Caps, perhaps the field mushrooms, and also the puffball. It would be a pity to disguise the natural flavours of morel and chanterelle, for example.

1 onion	*2 tablespoons chutney*
butter	*salt*
1 teaspoon flour	*1 pint stock*
2 tablespoons curry powder	*1 dozen mushrooms*

Fry an onion in butter. Then, mix in a cup the flour and curry powder and stir this into the butter and onion. Add some Indian chutney – or if you have none on hand any kind of so-called chutney or hot pickled stuffs – salt, and a pint of stock or bouillon or, if you have neither, milk. Cook gently fifteen minutes. Then add a dozen or so mushrooms, whole or sliced as you prefer, and simmer for about half an hour. If the sauce is very liquid remove the lid to let it evaporate, and serve on rice when the whole is of a good consistency. This is an excellent dish to serve to one's vegetarian friends.

Mushrooms make a fine addition to eggs done in almost any style, including, of course, mushroom omelette. Here are two different ways of preparing it:

MUSHROOM OMELETTE 1

Slice some mushrooms and fry lightly in seasoned butter. Make your omelette as you will. Let us say you beat your yolks and

whites separately, then fold the one into the other. Cook the omelette quickly, covered. When ready, put the mushrooms on one half, fold over, and serve on a hot plate.

MUSHROOM OMELETTE 2

Cut the mushrooms into small pieces. When the eggs have been beaten, add the mushrooms to them and cook your omelette.

Here are two of Elizabeth Raffald's recipes from her book, *The Experienced English House-Keeper:* For the Use and Ease of Ladies, House-keepers, Cooks etc. (For in those days you could not be both a cook *and* a lady!) Since the book was written in 1769, it is filled with those lisping words – like Mufhrooms and Tofling Pans – peculiar to those days. We reproduce them in modern print.

TO STEW MUSHROOMS

"Take large Buttons, wipe them with a wet Flannel, put them in a Stew Pan with a little Water, let them stew a quarter of an hour, then put in a little Salt, work a little Flour and Butter to make it as thick as Cream, let it boil five minutes, when you dish it up, put two large Spoonfuls of Cream mixed with the yolk of an egg, shake it over the fire about a minute or two, but don't let it boil for fear of curdling; put sippet round the inside of the rim of the dish, and not toasted, and serve it up. It is proper for a side dish, or a corner for dinner."

I doubt if that recipe could be improved. A sippet, by the way, is a small piece of bread soaked in liquid, or fried. Here is another pleasing recipe of hers:

TO MAKE MUSHROOM LOAVES

"Take small Buttons, wash them as for Pickling, put them in a Tossing Pan with a little white Bread Crumbs that have been boiled half an Hour in Water, then boil the mushrooms in the Bread and Water five Minutes, thicken with Flour and Butter and two Spoonfuls of Cream but no Yolks of Eggs, put in a little Salt then take five small French Rolls, make Holes in the Tops of them about the size of a Shilling and scrape out all the Crumb and put in your Mushrooms; stick a Bay Leaf on the Top of every Roll. Five is a handsome Dish for Dinner, and three for Supper."

Mushrooms are also an added attraction in a pilaf or any rice dish, or in the meat sauce of a spaghetti.

SAUCE FOR SPAGHETTI OR NOODLES

1 quart or more of mushrooms	*1 can tomatoes*
	sweet basil
clove of garlic	*cayenne*
4 tablespoons olive oil	*salt*

Wash and slice the mushrooms. Brown the garlic in the oil. Add the mushrooms. Simmer ten minutes. Add the tomatoes, stir and add flavourings. Cover. Simmer an hour, stirring occasionally. Pour over the hot spaghetti.

ANOTHER SAUCE

1 cup mushrooms	*1 cup stock (or water)*
1½ tablespoons fat	*1 tablespoon flour*
1 onion	

Skin and chop the mushrooms. Fry. Add the chopped onion. Lift out the mushrooms and onions. Mix the flour into the fat,

add the stock, and return the mushrooms and onions to the pan. Simmer gently.

MORE INTERESTING SAUCE

mushrooms	1 cup red wine
butter	1 cup stock
1 tablespoon flour	

Prepare some mushrooms, peeling them and slicing thick. Now, make a sauce by melting a piece of butter and stirring a tablespoon of flour about in it, vigorously. Then add a cup of red wine. Get it nicely stirred and mixed, after which put in your mushrooms, cook a couple of minutes and add a cupful of stock. This will make a delicious sauce to go with ham or the fish that you caught. To make it richer and more delicious you can work on it some more yet. Take two eggs and a half a cup of cream. Have the sauce heating very slowly, add the eggs and cream, and stir until it is all heated, without boiling.

MUSHROOM FRITTERS 1

2 cups mushrooms	½ cup milk
1 cup flour	1 egg, well beaten
1½ teaspoons baking	juice of half a lemon
powder	4 to 6 tablespoons
½ teaspoon salt	butter or oil
pepper	

Sift the dry ingredients. Make a hole in the middle, put in the egg, mix and add the milk.

Cut up the mushrooms fairly small, and cook them for a few minutes in lemon juice and water, just enough to keep them from burning. Put the mushrooms into the batter and drop by the spoonful into the hot butter or oil.

MUSHROOM FRITTERS 2

These are lighter and puffier than the others, but must be fried in deep fat.

Start your preparation an hour before you need the fritters.

Marinate as many small mushrooms as you desire fritters, in oil, pepper and salt for an hour.

½ cup of flour	salt
¼ cup water	1 egg separated
2 teaspoons salad oil	fat for deep frying
2 tablespoons brandy	mushrooms

Put into a basin the flour, water, salad oil and brandy, with a pinch of salt. Beat very well indeed, making sure there are no lumps, and that it is very smooth. Then stir in the egg yolk, and beat again for two or three minutes. Leave this for an hour or so. At the end of that time, beat up the egg white to a froth and lightly fold it into the batter.

Have ready a pan of deep fat. Dip a mushroom into the batter and drop it into the fat. Remove as soon as it turns golden, drain, and sprinkle with salt. Serve as hot as possible, naturally.

STUFFING

You can see how extremely useful the edible fungus is and how lucky you are to come across some on your country walk or drive. Another use to which they may be put is stuffing anything from tomatoes to turkeys.

STUFFING FOR PANCAKES

Pancakes that are to be stuffed must of course be very thin, not the half-inch-thick kind one gets in a restaurant which are all very well in their place, I suppose, but this is not their place.

pancake batter	butter
a dozen mushrooms	salt and pepper

Make your pancakes not too large and very thin, by pouring a small amount of runny batter onto the frying pan, then tipping it around so that the batter spreads out thinly and evenly. At the same time, be cooking your mushrooms, chopped up, in butter and seasoning. Now put a portion of the mushrooms on each pancake, which you then roll up. You can keep them hot by putting them in an oven dish in a warm oven.

I think you will like them served with a bowl of sour cream.

MUSHROOM AND WILD RICE STUFFING

Brown lightly in butter two cups of mushrooms, sliced. Toss them with one cup of cooked wild rice and a tablespoon of chopped onion. Bind with an egg and two tablespoons of orange juice. Add salt and pepper to taste.

MUSHROOM-STUFFED TOMATOES

6 large tomatoes
a dozen or so mushrooms
butter
1 tablespoon flour

1½ cups rich milk
salt and pepper
nutmeg or cheese, grated

Scoop out six large tomatoes. Fry your mushrooms for about five minutes and then remove from the pan. Stir the flour into the heated butter or oil and then slowly stir in the milk. Season. Simmer the mushrooms in this sauce until it is nice and thick. Stuff the tomatoes with it, sprinkling the tops with grated nutmeg or grated cheese. Bake for ten minutes in the oven.

STUFFING FOR TURKEY OR DOMESTIC DUCK

2 cups mushrooms
butter
1½ cups breadcrumbs
1 or 2 eggs

seasoning – salt, pepper,
and a tablespoon of
chopped parsley

Sauté the mushrooms, chopped. Mix with the breadcrumbs. Add an egg or two and plenty of seasoning, and stuff your bird.

MUSHROOM SALAD

Raw mushrooms are a dish that very few people in this country indulge in. Yet raw mushrooms can make a delicious dish and the Italians know this very well. A salad of tossed raw mushrooms makes a worthy ending to a veal scaloppine, for example.

Wash and peel your mushrooms. Slice nice and thin. Pour over them a dressing of olive oil in which garlic has been sitting, salt, pepper and a few drops of lemon juice. Let them sit in this for a few hours, tossing occasionally, before serving them.

Sometimes a couple of mushrooms, thinly sliced and added to a salad of greens, make a pleasant diversion.

Or, sauté them, chill, and marinate in a French dressing.

SNACKS

MUSHROOMS IN CREAM

Cut mushrooms in thin slices. Cook slowly fifteen minutes in a tablespoon or so of butter. Add a quarter-pint of thick cream, pepper and salt. Cook slowly ten minutes longer.

MUSHROOMS WITH TOMATOES

1 dozen small ripe tomatoes   *butter*
breadcrumbs   *garlic juice*
salt and pepper   *grated cheese*

Cut the tomatoes in halves. Roll them in the pepper-and-salted breadcrumbs. Melt some butter in a large frying pan or chafing dish, add a few drops of garlic juice, and brown the tomatoes on both sides. Now add your mushrooms, as many as you want,

more butter if you need it, and salt and pepper. Sprinkle with breadcrumbs and cheese. Cover and simmer for a few minutes.

This is a delicious snack served on toast, or a very nice side vegetable dish.

To make a heavenly aroma as well as flavour, fry some garlic, slivered, in butter. Add sliced mushrooms, and bacon if you like. When they are fried, add a cupful or so of red wine. Turn the heat up strongly for one minute watching it carefully, then turn down and simmer for ten minutes. Delicious hot or cold.

I want to give you a recipe from one of my favourite recipe books, Richard Dolby's *Cook's Dictionary*, published in 1830.

MUSHROOMS EN CANNELLON

Chop some mushrooms into dice, put them into a stew pan, with sliced parsley, scallions, shallots, and some butter; when a little browned, add stock, pepper and salt; let it simmer till the mushrooms are done, and the sauce pretty thick, then put in the yolks of three eggs and a little lemon juice; set it by to cool; in the meantime, roll some paste very thin, cut it in pieces, in each of which put some of the above, moisten the edges, and roll them up into the form of short sausages, flour and fry them.

PRESERVING MUSHROOMS AGAINST WINTER USE

TO DRY THEM

See that they are clean. Then put into a warm oven for an entire morning. If you leave the oven door open to provide circulation, you could have a hotter oven which would be slightly quicker.

If you have the space and the weather, you can also dry them in the open air, laying them on a screen in the sunshine.

Put the dried mushrooms into sterilized, dry jars and seal them tightly.

MUSHROOMS PICKLED

1 to 2 pounds mushrooms *½ teaspoon tarragon*
1 cup vinegar *1 teaspoon salt*
mace *1 tablespoon sugar*
pepper

Cut your mushrooms into slices or keep whole, depending on the size and species.

Cook the vinegar, mace, pepper, tarragon, salt and sugar together, and bring to a boil. Put your mushrooms into this and cook slowly for three minutes. Lift the mushrooms out and put into sterilized jars. Boil up the vinegar again and pour over the mushrooms. Cap.

A FRIEND'S RECIPE FOR PRESERVING MUSHROOMS

Make a brine of salt and water. Fill glass jars with your mushrooms, pour the brine over. Slightly unscrew the tops to let the air out. Put the jars in a water bath, covering it and bringing to a boil.

Take the jars out, screw them tight, and turn them upside down.

You might also be intrigued to make some

MUSHROOM POWDER

This would make an unusual gift, a small jar of it being quite sufficient, for it is to be used as a flavouring agent.

After the mushrooms are dried whole (using method above), set them before the fire till crisp. Then grind and sift them through a fine sieve, preserve in small, tightly corked bottles.

CHAPTER 10

Wild fowl

Canada goose
                    pheasant
ruffed grouse
                    woodcock
quail

Wild fowl

> "When bass, fish and pigeons (and wild duck) were produced, boiled and fried, they looked so appetisants, smelt so savoury – that I soon forgot all my sentimental pity for the victims."
>
> Anna Jameson: *Winter Studies and Summer Rambles* (1838)

A matter of lively controversy among connoisseurs in regard to cooking game birds, especially ducks, is whether to cook them briefly or for a long time, and whether or not to stuff them.

I am of the cook long and the stuff-if-you-like schools, though any bird which is not stuffed will need much less time to cook through than the stuffed one. Also, the dark-fleshed birds should be rosy rare. Having shot your bird, hang it by the head in a cool place, undrawn. A couple of days should suffice for ducks and snipe, but several (four or five) for quail and grouse.

Wild duck

"– we soon sat down to a sumptuous feast, consisting of a brace of fine fat wood ducks and fried black bass."

Samuel Strickland: *Twenty-seven Years in the Bush* (1853)

ROAST DUCK

duck	*half an apple*
1 stick of celery	*half an orange*
1 whole onion	*2 slices of bacon*

Pluck your wild duck, singe and clean him. Then try to locate and remove all the shot. (This goes for all game birds of course.) A sharply pointed knife will help you dig them out.

Put the celery stick, onion, and apple and orange halves into the cavity. Salt and pepper the skin, lay the bacon over the breast, and put the bird into a baking pan with a small amount of water. Cover, or lay over it a well-greased piece of brown paper. Cook in a 350 degree oven about one and half hours.

or

Cook uncovered for 20 minutes in a hot oven (500 degrees).

If the duck has been kept in the freezer for some time, it is not only an elegant gesture, but also a practical one, to pour a liqueur glass of brandy over the bird and light it at the moment of serving. Since the fat on the bird does not freeze, it tends to become rancid, and the brandy happily burns away some of this rancidity.

Serve the duck, if possible, with wild rice and chokecherry jelly. Two ducks serve three people very nicely.

Woodcock and snipe

If woodcock had partridge's breast
'Twould be the best bird ever dressed.

Woodcock and snipe are dark meat birds. Traditionally, they
are not drawn but cooked with the entrails in. I have not had
them prepared this way so cannot comment – except to say
that it would certainly be *easier*.

ROAST WOODCOCK (OR SNIPE)

woodcock, 1 or more   *salt and pepper*
per person   *butter*

Having plucked and cleaned (or not, as you wish) the woodcock, sprinkle inside and out with salt and pepper. Rub with

butter and add a piece of butter to the pan. Put in a hot oven (450 degrees) for about ten minutes. Then reduce to medium (350 degrees) for another ten or fifteen minutes, basting every five minutes with butter.

It is usually sent to the table on slices of fried bread or toast.

BROILED WOODCOCK

woodcock	slice of toast for each bird
butter	slices of lemon
salt and pepper	

Rub with butter or olive oil, salt and pepper inside and out and broil 10 minutes on each side, under a medium flame. Turn them often to get browned all over.

Serve with slices of lemon and toast.

Quail and partridge

Quail and partridge, being white meat fowl, will take a longer cooking than other game fowl.

ROAST QUAIL OR PARTRIDGE

birds	powdered ginger
1 strip of bacon for each bird	flour for gravy
½ cup white wine (or water)	

Having seasoned the birds, lay strips of bacon along the breasts, put them in the pan and pour half a cup of water or white wine around them. Roast for an hour to an hour and a quarter at 375 degrees, basting every fifteen minutes. A few minutes before removing from the oven, sprinkle them lightly with ginger.

Thicken the pan juice to make a gravy to serve with them, adding, if you have them, the liver and kidney chopped up.

QUAIL EN CASSEROLE

quail	*1 cup white wine or light*
butter	*sherry*
salt and pepper	*1 cup mushrooms, sliced*
cinnamon	

Melt some butter in a large frying pan and quickly brown the quail in it. Then lay the birds in a casserole, add salt and pepper and a pinch of cinnamon. Pour in the cup of wine or sherry and add a small chunk of butter. Then add the cup of mushrooms. Cover and cook three-quarters to one hour in a moderate (350 degrees) oven.

You may wish to thicken the sauce slightly, or leave it as it is to be sopped up with bits of French bread.

Grouse

Many hunter-gourmets insist that the ruffed grouse (colloquially and incorrectly known as partridge) is *the* game bird. How, I wonder, does one choose?

ROAST GROUSE

grouse	*1 cup red wine*
butter	*(or water)*
bacon	*flour for gravy*

Put a walnut of butter inside the grouse and cover the outside with strips of bacon. Salt and pepper. Add a cup of water or red

wine to the roasting pan. Cook in a hot oven (425 degrees) for twenty-five minutes, basting frequently with the liquid.

Thicken the liquid with flour to make a gravy. This recipe is also suitable for prairie chicken.

BROILED GROUSE

Split the birds down the back and flatten them. Rub all over with butter and broil for fifteen minutes on each side, basting several times with more melted butter.

This may also be used for mourning dove, provided you can bring yourself to eat mourning dove, and provided, of course, that it is on the game list, which it is but rarely.

Pheasant

I like pheasant stuffed. Hence:

ROAST STUFFED PHEASANT

1 cup onions, diced small	1 egg, beaten
1 cup celery, diced small	seasonings
1 cup soft breadcrumbs	¾ cup milk

Mix the onions, celery and breadcrumbs well together, then add the egg and seasonings and mix some more. Add enough of the milk to make a wet dressing. Stuff the bird until he is bursting and then sew or tie him up. Cover with the bacon strips.

Roast in a covered pan in a medium oven (350 degrees) for an hour. Then remove the cover and take the bacon out; turn the oven up to 450 degrees and cook for another fifteen minutes or until the skin is brown and crisp.

A traditional sauce to serve with roast pheasant (and also grouse) is bread sauce. There is, of course, no earthly reason to serve it if you don't like. A rich brown gravy is perfectly adequate.

BREAD SAUCE

Put one medium-sized onion into a pint of milk, with salt and pepper, and bring to a boil. Then add one cup of white dry breadcrumbs. Cook together about five minutes to obtain a thickish sauce. Add a tablespoon of butter, taste for flavour, remove the onion, and the sauce is ready to serve.

Wild goose

For those lucky enough to go up to the northern feeding grounds in autumn – or to know someone who does.

ROAST GOOSE

For the stuffing:
1 cup breadcrumbs
1 cup chopped walnuts
1 cup prunes, partly
  cooked and stoned
½ cup celery
2 onions
salt and pepper
milk

For the skin:
1 tablespoon sugar
½ teaspoon each of ginger,
  cinnamon, ground cloves

Add only enough milk to the stuffing to keep it from falling apart completely. The goose is a fat bird, and the stuffing will be moistened during the cooking. You may prefer to bake the stuffing in a separate dish for that reason.

When you have cleaned the goose, be sure to save the liver as a tidbit for another meal.

In a cup mix the sugar and spices. Put the goose in its pan and sprinkle the mixture over the skin. Roast the bird for 2½ to 3 hours. It is advisable to pour off the fat half an hour before the goose is finished cooking. Potatoes, put into the same pan as the goose, cook beautifully in this fat.

Or wild goose can be stuffed with mushroom and wild rice. (See page 173).

CURRIED LEFT-OVER GOOSE

2 or 3 onions
butter
2 tablespoons curry
  powder

1 green apple
1 cup beef broth or
  consommé

Cut up the onions very fine, and fry them well in butter. Remove them, and stir into the remaining melted butter the two tablespoons of curry powder, mixing it well, but being careful not to burn it. Chop the apple very fine. Add this, together with the broth and the onions, to the curry paste, stirring it all well. Add salt to taste. Let this simmer, covered, for an hour or two. Cut your cold goose remains into small pieces and add them half an hour before serving.

I like to add a handful of raisins or well-stalked currants also. This is not a mild curry, but if you like it *really* hot, use four tablespoons of curry and a little cayenne.

It should be served, of course, on or with rice. In separate dishes you might like Indian chutney, grated coconut toasted in

the oven, and bananas cut up into tiny cubes with lemon juice squeezed over them.

The 'left-over' recipes are included under wild goose, because you are more likely to have left-overs of goose than of the smaller game birds. However, any game may be used, and indeed, several kinds at once may be used in the soups – if anyone is fortunate enough to *have* several kinds at once.

GAME SOUP 1

Put bones, with any meat, skin or stuffing left, into a pot with water to cover. Season. Bring it to a boil and then simmer for at least an hour, preferably two. Strain, putting the broth back into the saucepan. Pick out any solid, boneless, fatless pieces of meat, cut them up and return them to the broth. Heat again before serving.

GAME SOUP 2

remains of birds
2 turnips
3 onions stuck with a few
  cloves
3 pints stock or water

2 egg yolks
1 cup cream
1 glass red wine

Remove any good meat left on the bones. Then put the bones, turnips, onions and stock or water into a pot. Simmer for a couple of hours, until the vegetables are tender. Remove the bones and press what is left through a sieve.

When you are about to serve the soup, add the bits of meat, the well-beaten egg yolks, the cream and the red wine. Heat gently, but do not boil.

Wild pigeons

PALPATION* OF PIGEONS

(From *The Noble Book of Cookery*, printed in 1500)

Take mushrooms, palates**, oysters, sweetbread, fry them in butter; put all into strong gravy; give them a heat over the fire, and thicken up with an egg and a bit of butter; then half roast six or eight pigeons, and lay them in a crust of forcemeat, as follows: – Scrape a pound of veal and two pounds of marrow, and beat together in a stone mortar, after 'tis shed very fine; then season it well with salt, pepper, and spice, and put in hard eggs, anchovies and oysters; beat all together, and make the lid and side of your pye with it. First lay in thin crust in your pattepan***, then put on your forced meat, then lay in exceeding thin crust over them, then put in your pigeons and other ingredients with a little butter at the top; bake it two hours.

BROILED PIGEONS

a pigeon a person	*rice*
butter	*currants*
salt and pepper	

Cook the rice while the pigeons are being broiled. They should both be ready at the same time.

---

* No, I haven't the foggiest notion what this means.
** Nor this.
*** See Beatrix Potter.

Pluck and draw young pigeons. Split them down the back and season all over with salt and pepper. Rub them with butter and lay under the grill. Turn them in five minutes, rubbing the other side with butter. Turn once or twice more, until they are evenly browned and cooked.

Add a handful of stalked currants to the rice. Spread the rice on a platter, lay your sizzling pigeons on it, and pour over them some more melted, bubbling butter.

PIGEON PIE

½ dozen pigeon breasts	bay leaf
mushrooms	thyme
1 or 2 onions	puff pastry
1 or 2 carrots	

Bone the breasts and cover them with water. Add the onions, the carrots sliced thinly lengthwise, the bay leaf and thyme. Bring this to the boil, then simmer, covered, for an hour or more, until tender.

Pour off the stock and thicken with flour, adding salt to taste. Roll out the puff paste and line a casserole dish with it. Bake. When it is done, put in the pigeons and other ingredients, pour the gravy over them and cover with the remaining paste. Bake in a hot (450 degrees) oven until the crust is browned.

STUFFED PIGEONS

4 pigeons, picked and cleaned	1 can of sour cherries, drained
melted butter	

Rub the pigeons all over with butter and salt, and stuff them with the cherries. Roast them for three quarters of an hour in a 350 degree oven, basting occasionally with melted butter.

As I write, the snow is shrinking in the woods, sap is dripping into the buckets hanging on the sugar maples, and the rainbow trout are up in the shallows of the rivers, spawning. The harvest of wild foods from field and woods, river and stream begins, generously, very early in the year and goes on munificently until almost the end of the year. And there are, of course, many more wild plants – and animals – than have been mentioned in this book.

I hope you discover and enjoy them all.

Index

WILD PLUMS
IN BRANDY